Born For More

One woman's inspiring journey from abject poverty, death and despair to living a life of dreams and fulfillment

Neecol Resnin

Published by
RockStar Publishing House
32129 Lindero Canyon Road, Suite 205
Westlake Village, CA 91361
www.rockstarpublishinghouse.com

Copyright © 2017 by: Neecol Resnin

All rights reserved. No part of this book may be reproduced or transmitted in any form or by any means, electronic or mechanical, including photocopying, recording, or by any information storage and retrieval system, without the written permission of the Publisher, except where permitted by law.

Manufactured in the United States of America, or in the United Kingdom when distributed elsewhere.

Author: Resnin, Neecol
Title of Book: Born for More
ISBN:
　　Paperback: 978-1-938015-28-1
　　eBook: 978-1938015-29-8

Cover design by: Joe Potter
Cover photo by: Val Westover
Interior design: Scribe Inc.

Warning-Disclaimer
The purpose of the book is to educate and entertain. The author or publisher does not guarantee that anyone following the techniques, suggestions, tips, ideas or strategies will become successful. The author and publisher shall have neither liability nor responsibility to anyone with respect to any loss or damage caused, or alleged to be caused, directly or indirectly by the information contained in this book.

Author's URL: www.bornformore.com

CONTENTS

	Foreword	vii
	Introduction—Moments Before I Died	1
1	Your Life Matters	5
2	You Are Qualified	9
3	You Are Worth Loving	17
4	Wake Up Your Courageous Self	23
5	Your Desires Matter	29
6	Get Up, Get Away, Get Going	35
7	You Can Overcome Any Addiction	43
8	Conquering Breast Cancer	49
9	Change Your Script: Change Your Life	55
10	Forgiveness: The Key to Mastery	59
11	Complete Restoration Awaits You	63
12	My Personal Creed	69
	Epilogue	71
	Appendix A—Inspiration	73
	Appendix B—Resources for Recovering from Addiction	85
	Appendix C—My Tips for Coping with Breast Cancer	89

ACKNOWLEDGEMENT

My first thanks is to God, who has kept me, held me, comforted me and guided me through each challenge, through stormy waters and into green pastures of peace and prosperity.

To Louise Hay, my first teacher of love, and transformation. Thanks for believing in me, encouraging me way back when on Berkeley Street in West L.A. You are the beginning of all of this.

This book would truly not be possible without the help, love and support of Maryann Ehmann. Thank you for believing in me and going the distance with me. You are a magnificent divine connection, a mentor and a friend. I love you so much.

I want to thank Craig Duswalt for creating Rockstar Marketing Seminar and Mastermind Bootcamp. My life has never been the same since attending your seminars.

To Maurice DiMino for sharing your million dollar method of public speaking.

To James Malinchak for sharing your Big Money Speaker genius with us.

To my good friend, Sy Richardson, thanks for remaining true to yourself and your art. I love you my friend.

To the late great Chris Hicks, my mentor and friend, you helped me in more ways than we will ever know. You were sent from God.

A grateful and heartfelt thanks goes out to my family and my children, who have taught me what unconditional love is all about.

To my best friend and sister, Rosa Allen, who has always been my cheerleader and embraced all of my wonderful and far out ideas. Thank you for your wedge of love.

To my childhood friends: Shirley McFarland and Vera Pitts. Wow, we are so much better because of our friendship. My life is enriched with the wonderful joy your friendship brings. To Betty Jean, you are such a caring friend who has always been full of helpful information. To Betty Girl, the two of us escaped gun fire by jumping out of a second floor window with two kids. Are we super heroes? To Judy Lee, my dear friend.

I am so thankful for all of the people who have crossed my path and inspired me, helped me, encouraged me. If I have not named you, you are important to me. May this book inspire you.

To Janice Miller and Grace Harper for getting me to the hospital just in time. To Johnnie Latson and Janice for caring so much about me even when I was confused and outrageous. Johnnie, your words of compassion are with me today.

To Karen Strauss and the publishing company, thank you for your patience and guidance.

To Thyra Cushingberry, thanks for your friendship.

To Kenneth and Gloria Copeland for all that you do. Your ministry inspires me. I am one in your million.

FOREWORD

If you ever question your lifestyle, your purpose on earth, not knowing which way to continue, and you haven't found your sunny side of the street, but you believe there is a way, then *Born For More* will enlighten you.

This book will open up your heart and mind to realize that life is more than a line of scrimmage. Neecol Resnin tells her life adventure with honesty and straight forwardness. She doesn't omit those awkward or embarrassing moments. It's one of those books that you can't put down until you finished it.

I have known Neecol from our college years and witnessed some of her decisions, but I didn't realize how extremely broken her wings were. Nevertheless, she never quit flapping away.

After reading *Born For More*, my eyes grew teary when I read a quote from her book, "I have gone from victim to victor. From suicide to success." Her book is about prayer, hope and persistence. It's about life. It's a celebration of God's grace and never giving up.

Because we are *Born For More*.

Love you, my dear friend,
Sy Richardson,
Actor, Author, Director

INTRODUCTION

Moments Before I Died

"Her pressure is falling. Sixty. Forty. There's no pressure! I need the paddles!"

"Stand back!"

"Try again!"

"Again!"

What is happening? Oh my goodness, there I am! My body is so wrinkled, crumpled. I look so bad. Where am I? It's a hospital.

That is me down there. I can see the lights, the doctors, and the nurses! I am all hooked up to things, looking so lifeless. I hear them. I see them. Oh, oh, my body jumped! They are trying to make my heart start.

I can see myself, but really, I am here. Below is just my body. It looks empty. So frail, so fragile. The doctors are saying that I have no heartbeat. I see them, but they can't see me. They're trying again. They are working on my body, but I am not in it. I do not feel anything.

"Here I am! Up here!" *I call out to them, but they cannot hear me.*

My body is not the real me! Am I dead? I can still think and see. And they are still working on me.

I need that body. The only way I can have what I want in life will have to be in that body. It can't exist without me. Without it, I cannot exist. Goodness, I can see that I should have been nicer to my body.

"Hey! Here I am! I'm still here!"

* * *

That was my last thought for the next approximately sixty hours. When I came to, I realized that I was in the hospital and in the same body that I had been looking at. I felt terribly weak, but I also wanted to get out of that place. My first attempt at ending my painful life had failed.

The voices of desperation that had raced through my head in the minutes before I lost consciousness came back to me:

God, I am in despair. I am so alone.

To the outside world, I look great. Inside, there is only darkness and despair. There is no one here to help me. Everyone looks to me, but who can I look to?

No one knows of this lonely desperate place that I live in. Secretly, I pretend that I am OK. I wish someone else knew how much I am hurting. I wish someone could hold me, hug me, help me get through this pain and take me from this darkness. I have drugs. I can just take them all and end it.

I've always tried to reach out to anyone who appeared desperate and in need of help. People have me as a resource. But today I don't want to give any more. I am tired. My fire is gone. I am such a failure. I may look good on the outside, but I hate me on the inside. I cannot help me. I have failed me. I am in so much pain.

I feel like I balance between pretending and believing, looking to others like I can do all things, but never really feeling like I accomplish anything. I feel like something is terribly wrong with me. Other people have jobs, nice cars. What's wrong with me? Why don't I get the things I want?

Father, please help me escape this hell I'm in—escape the hate that lives in me. I want to be your child, but I'm told that it's too late—backsliders don't get a second chance.

Will someone help me or will I die? I want to be at the top of the world and teach the world it can be done.

I have given wisdom to my friends, inspiring and motivating them to help set their worlds free. I taught them to believe in themselves— and they did; they took to the winds of success. Believing in me (their friend) enriched their lives. Now they have gone on, living a richer and more meaningful life.

And I am still here. I lie in utter distress and despair.

Two of my friends took their own life. They are missed. They were mourned. They are free from this dark world.

I will take this last bottle of pills to end it all. One hundred pills away from freedom. And then I, too, will be free.

Take away my pain. I have broken my own heart. I've destroyed all my hopes and dreams, all that I wanted to achieve. I must punish me. I am so sorry to everyone I hurt. Sorry I failed you all. Sorry I could not have been better. I am sorry. I can't handle my life anymore.

CHAPTER 1

Your Life Matters

As I lay in the hospital bed reflecting on what had happened, I realized that this had been one of my darkest hours. My desire had been to die, and I set out to try. There was so much pain. I felt that I was a failure to myself and everyone else. I could nourish others but did not know how to give myself that same kindness. I could help others, encourage them, even save them from destruction, but I couldn't help myself. There were too many failures; too many good starts only to end with no measurable success. Nothing. I felt like a fake and was afraid that everyone would know it.

How did I get to this low point? What circumstances drove me to this dramatic action? The external factors were that my world had collapsed. My lover left to be with my best friend. The internal factor was that I believed I was not good enough. My job ended, which caused me to fear I would have no money for rent and be kicked out onto the street.

After I was revived and medically stable, I still wanted to die. When the doctor asked, "Why did you want to kill yourself?" I uttered my standard response—weakly, but without hesitation, "Because I hate myself, and I'll try to do it again. Just let me out of here." And out I went; I had no medical insurance.

I would like to say that it was the one and only time I tried to end my life, but sadly, it was not. I had several more encounters— three that landed me in the hospital.

After being diagnosed with breast cancer, I felt alone and very depressed. Although I told my friends that everything was OK, I took an overdose of pills. Somewhere in between the time I fell asleep and before the ambulance arrived, one of my friends called me (I have no recollection of this) and later told me that I sounded so bad that she called 911.

When I woke up, I was in intensive care and was told that I had been in a coma for over a week. I was confused, deadened from medication and brain fog, and *angry*. Again, my attempt did not work out as I had planned. The psychiatrist on duty decided I was still a risk to myself and placed a psychiatric hold on me. He ordered a transfer to a psychiatric hospital for treatment and observation for seventy-two hours—a 5150 hold in California.

Although still weak with my spirit broken, I still wanted to die and intended to try again. Transported by ambulance, with restraints on my wrists and ankles, I could not get up and run. After I was evaluated, I was escorted to my room; I was on the locked unit and the only people who could leave were the staff who had keys. There were no windows in the room, only in the area near the nurse's station. I had previously been admitted to the psych unit in another hospital for a suicide attempt, so I understood that I was really locked in.

Frustrated and frail, I opened a drawer in my room and saw a Bible. Still in emotional pain, I opened the Bible. I scoffed, "What is this Bible supposed to do for patients in mental distress and locked in a psych ward?!" Nevertheless, I randomly opened the book and my eyes fell on this passage: "I shall not die, but live, and declare the works of the Lord" (Ps 118:17, KJV)—*my divine lifeline*.

What? How could this have happened? This Bible, this book, had no power or ability. Yet, when I turned to the passage, I knew immediately that it was a direct message from God to me. In spite of my own desperation, my own struggles, my own pain, God wanted me to live and not die. He did not want me to destroy the vision He had for me. The plans He had for my life were obviously vastly different from the ones that I had, which had landed me in the psychiatric hospital. I had a message that I was to live and not die.

I believe that God has a message for each of us. That biblical passage was my personal message; it was my lifeline. I now believed there was a reason for me to be alive, but how? How was I to "live and not die" and live out God's plan for my life?

In the weeks after my release, I contacted a couple of people that I had met at a church I had recently attended for a bit. Both of them were so positive. There was caring in their voices. It seemed that this might be my link to getting better.

God told me that He wanted me to be alive by divinely intervening and saving my life. It was a sign of His love and favor. I knew it. I could not go back now. I had to fight to live and overcome those places that needed healing. I needed to figure out why I should be alive—what purpose might be out there?

It has been years since these incidents occurred and I thought that suicide was my only option. Thank God I was wrong. I have learned how to love myself and find a life of purpose and freedom. I have completed two master degrees, have a job filled with purpose and meaning, and have children who I love and who love me.

* * *

I am sharing my story with you so that you can see how it is possible to rise above almost any hardship in life—as you will see, I've had a few. I want you to see the powerfully positive lessons that I have learned along the way; lessons that ultimately brought me out of despair and desperation into a life of purpose, success, and utter joy.

Finding my message reminded me of another message that God sent—to Noah. After forty days and forty nights of rain, God placed a rainbow in the sky as a promise that the world would not end in water. But it was also a promise that God's grace and favor lives with us, even when we feel we don't deserve it. In my weakest moment, in my darkest day, God was with me so that I could see the promise of His love and favor. He is still with me. It may not make me a millionaire or fill my every wish and desire, but His favor is a solid sign that I am here for a purpose. Still alive, I can achieve any dream. Dead, the story and dreams are gone forever.

I once heard Cher say, "I have been poor and now I am rich. Rich is better." Well, on a similar note, I have been at death's door, wanting to end my life, but now I am alive and well. Living is better.

You are also here for a purpose. You, too, can achieve any dream.

Your desire for a better life, a better job, more income, more or better anything (you fill in the blank) can be fulfilled. No matter how hopeless life may look, you have value and worth. Your life matters.

Your best life is waiting for you.

CHAPTER 2

You Are Qualified

All my life I have struggled against the *you're-not-qualified* script. Each of us has a story where the seeds of despair were planted, watered, and strengthened. For me growing up, the idea that I was not qualified for a good life was vividly, and often cruelly, demonstrated on a daily basis.

When I was little, my siblings and I lived with my grandparents, and my mother lived in St. Louis with other relatives. Eventually she got a better job and came back to get us, but my oldest sister remained living in the South with my grandparents.

My brother and I were headed for the big city! My grandmother spoke to us about the benefits of living in such a large city: Life would be much easier. Jobs would be more plentiful. There would be nice housing and free medical care for the poor and elderly. The good life was a state or two away. I was ready and excited to embrace this change with its promise of hope.

Unfortunately, the picture that had been painted did not turn out to be the reality. Life in St. Louis was not as I had hoped it would be. We shared an apartment building with several other tenants. To my dismay, I discovered we would be sharing the bathroom with all the other tenants in the building. I was not quite sure how this worked, but after a few people screamed, "Girl, you better get your black butt in line and wait for the bathroom like everyone else," I got the picture. I did not like it, but what could I do?

My brother, mother, and I (and soon-to-arrive baby sister) had two rooms to live in: the kitchen and the all-purpose room, which included my mother's bed, a couple of chairs, and a roll-away bed. Initially I slept with my mother unless it was the weekend or a ladies' night out at the club. Then her newly found boyfriend would come over and she would go into the kitchen, pull the curtain back (that separated the room), and the boyfriend would leave by seven or so the next morning.

I always faulted her for picking out the poorest, meanest boyfriends. I always thought that at least we should have gotten an ice cream cone or White Castle hamburgers as a benefit of the visits, but there was nothing. Mostly they enjoyed their liquor and a good time together, and then they were gone.

Winters in St. Louis could be very cold. There were always numerous reports of infants, small children, and the elderly who died each year due to some poor family not being able to afford to pay their gas bill in the dead of winter. When my mother could not afford to pay her gas bill, she would buy or negotiate a coal-burning stove (with no proper ventilation) in order for us to have some heat and warmth in the house. It doubled as a stove top, and our meals were cooked on this stove. (Eventually, a law was passed so that one's heat could not be shut off until spring if the bill was unpaid in the winter. However, the next winter, that family would not have heat unless their bill had been paid for in full before winter began.)

During this period of time, I was often sick with asthma, and my mother took me to a wonderful hospital—Homer G. Phillips Hospital in St. Louis. They heard me wheezing and struggling to breathe. I was hospitalized and treated for asthma several times during the winter months. Ah, what a relief it was. I had a warm place to stay, doctors and nurses to take care of me, and they would supply me with a toothbrush, which I was allowed to take home with me (yay!); deodorant; lotion; and, yes, Kleenex to wipe my constantly running eyes and nose. (Thanks to the roach- and rat-infested housing, I had severe allergies.)

We were poor and there was no way to dress it up.

Life was a series of battles. In addition to my battling for health or time in the bathroom, kids wanted to fight me because I was new. One day a group of girls spotted me in my classroom and threatened me by displaying their fists. Later, as I walked home alone, they jumped me, punching my arms, hitting me in the head, telling me they had to "teach me a lesson." To this day, I still don't know what that lesson was. Basically, I was new in the neighborhood and stood out; therefore, I was punished for it.

Other times they would want to fight me if I did well in school. Any time the teacher made a laudatory comment to one of us who had done something correctly, we were told, "You think you're better than the rest of us."

Some of the kids would tell me, "You stink!" (Actually, I did, but not by choice.) I did not like being told I was a smelly kid. When I would ask my mother for soap and deodorant, I was told the soap was for washing clothes. We could not afford toothpaste or toothbrushes, so I could rarely brush my teeth. If baking soda was available, we could use a washcloth or rag to clean them. At one point, I used Tide detergent to clean my face, brush my teeth, and clean the rest of my body, but I quickly developed a rash inside my mouth. My mother told me to just throw some water on my face.

At school, this battle continued. I had a fourth-grade teacher who called out everyone who smelled. Of course, I was one of the smelly ones. She would say, "Neecol, how often do you take a bath?" I never did, but I lied and told her I bathed twice a day. Nevertheless, she said, "You stink and you need to take a bath." The problem was that we did not have a bathtub—only a toilet. You did your business and then you vacated it for the next person. Didn't she understand that? We could not afford deodorant; we were too poor for hygiene. I wanted to tell her that so she would stop labeling me a dirty kid.

I promised myself when I grew up and became a teacher, I would have a hygiene kit in my desk for all the poor little kids who could not afford soap and deodorant. It would be our secret. I would give them permission to come into my classroom early, take their kit to the bathroom, clean up, and return the kit. No one would know their secret.

I learned early on that in order to survive, one had to take on many battles. Besides the ones about being new, stinky, or too smart, I had battles with the men in the neighborhood. They would whistle and said nasty things to innocent young girls. I also battled trying to win my mother's love and affection. She loved my brother, who was light skinned and good looking. They were so compatible—more like friends. Then there was the battle to have milk to drink or a hot lunch at school. My mother refused to sign papers for us to qualify for a hot lunch but gave us money for the milk. However, we had to take it home at lunch for my baby sister.

Clothing was another struggle. I had only two dresses and had to wear them all the time. I had one pair of underwear, maybe two, and both my shoes and socks had holes in them. Practically everything in life was a battle.

One day, the opportunity for all that to change presented itself! My mother told us that we might be able to get an apartment in the projects. She applied, and we eagerly waited. While many looked down on the projects, they were nirvana to us.

We were all excited because even though many poor people lived in the projects, they all had appropriate housing. If there were three kids, they would receive an apartment that would accommodate all of them. Girls would sleep in one room, and boys would have their own room. That meant my mother was going to have her own bedroom, my sister and I would share a bedroom, and my brother would have his own room. Three bedrooms in one apartment—it was a dream! And that was not all—we would also have a living room, a kitchen, and a bathroom with hot running water with a *bathtub and a sink*! We were all so excited; we would have a normal life. The utilities, lights, and gas were included in the rent. Oh the joy that thinking of our move brought us! We were happy and frequently talked about what we would do in our own rooms.

Finally, the letter from the housing authority arrived. We were so excited. As my mom read the letter out loud, I thought that she read it wrong. It said we were being denied housing (in the *low-income project for low-income families*) because our income was too *low* to qualify for low-income housing! A deadening silence fell upon all of us. I felt sick to my stomach.

Our dreams were crushed with the rejection letter. *We did not qualify*. In order to qualify for low-income housing, the monthly income needed to be a minimum of one hundred dollars. My mother's total income from welfare was ninety-two dollars per month. We were *eight dollars short* of having decent housing. The fact that we did not qualify was a pronouncement that we did not count.

I tried to talk to the social worker who came by the building to plead our cause, but she had no heart for us. She just kept repeating, "You don't qualify." I felt so hopeless. We all felt the pain. The belief that we were nobodies and that no one cared about us was becoming solidified.

Everything about life in St. Louis seemed to be a struggle. I longed for a life like my older sister had. She lived with my grandparents in a well-organized, warm, and comforting three-bedroom home in Arkansas. There was always plenty there. But this was not the life I lived. A bitterness of anger, jealousy, and despair took root and strengthened as the years went on. In spite of this building attitude and the obstacles placed in my way, deep down I knew that I had to get out. I had to find a different way to have a life. I knew I would find one. I clung to hope.

* * *

As a young girl, while life was telling me that I was not qualified for a good life, I did not initially accept this. I believe God put a seed of strength inside me—I came that way. I battled hard on every front, but the one battle that I needed to win most was the battle to believe that I had value, had worth, and was qualified.

When one believes this, something within finds a way. In spite of the hardness of life, I looked for opportunities to take care of myself and improve my state of being. I found a way to have a job and buy myself some of the needed things that a child should not have to think about: soap, deodorant, and even Kleenex.

I could not pretend circumstances were not as they were; I had to face life realistically. At times, I was in despair, but I could not let it define me. I could not give in to it. Keeping faith that things will get better was crucial to my very existence.

Frequently, one must actually admit defeat when it is blatant. Some doors do close and never open for you. But temporary failures and repeated setbacks can make one stronger and more determined to rise above the circumstances, even when it means walking out of the current situation.

While we did not qualify for low-income housing, I never gave up on qualifying for a better life. Temporarily the dark messages and defeat might take over, but underneath was that seed of strength—waiting for me to find it again.

As difficult as it is to believe, what I know now and what I sensed as a young girl is that no one is destined for a life of poverty, filth, neglect, or abuse just because they were raised in it. God has qualified each of us for a life that is more abundant.

Just as with me, God has planted a seed of strength in you. Nurture your hope, take your stand, and move forward, even if only one step at a time. Be determined that this current situation in your life is not permanent or final. The Bible says, "Ask, and it will be given to you; seek, and you will find; knock, and it will be opened to you" (Matt 7:7, NASB).

Do you feel that you do not qualify for something you desire in life? Can you identify what makes you feel this way? Are you eight dollars short of a dream for something more? Are you seeking a promotion in your career but not getting it? Are you stuck in a behavioral pattern? Is your income not adequate to meet your needs and those of your family? Are you a few feet away from a breakthrough that just never seems to come?

You *can* overcome your challenges. You may be in a place where your level of comfort is not what God designed for you, but it's OK to dream big. Believe that you can achieve your goals and you will receive more in your life.

Look around you. If someone else has a success story, use it as a model; it's an example that you can have one as well. Find ways to encourage yourself. You know yourself better than anyone. I believe you can have and achieve whatever you want in life.

Others may disqualify you, but life does not. God does not. God's plan is for you to have an abundant life. He considers you His own and that more than qualifies you for every blessing life has to offer.

Go for it!

CHAPTER 3

You Are Worth Loving

Each of us yearns to be loved. We are made to love and be loved. God is love and it is His express purpose that we experience genuine and true, unconditional love. Each of us is worth loving!

I, too, was worth loving, but as you read in chapter 1, I didn't love myself. Indeed, I hated myself. No matter how hard I tried in life, no matter how many others I helped, I still hated myself. Self-hatred is such a painful mental state that grips a soul. For some in this state, it can be inconceivable that life can be anything but pain; self-hatred produces immense pain.

Where does self-hatred come from? I don't believe that any child enters life hating him- or herself. They must be taught to do so. I also believe it is rare that parents don't love their children. Parents may be frustrated, struggling, or even have personality clashes with their children, which may cause a child to get the impression that he or she is not really loved. Sometimes it is out of love and concern that parents express their fear in some negative, shaming way, again causing the child to feel they are not loved. Worry wrongly expressed can make a child feel rejected.

For years I was convinced that my mother hated me and that I was worthy of such hatred. Why did I think that? Because she often told me. I will never forget the look on her face and the darkness in her eyes as she revealed that she hated the fact that she had ever had me. After the initial thrust into my heart, there would be many other times when the knife would be twisted, only to penetrate deeper levels of my being. Eventually, I believed the lie that I was unlovable and worthy of hatred. I perpetuated this lie by thoroughly hating myself.

I do not wish to blame her, for she did the best she could with what she had. She had a dire, poverty-stricken life. It was hard and she hated it. What I had to do with the quality of her life, other than being another mouth to feed, I'm not sure. She seemed to prefer my siblings, and so I assumed there was something about me that warranted her feelings, but I never really knew why.

It is my experience that in all situations, no matter how oppressive, there is always a silver lining. While I adopted the hate and pain my mother felt, it also propelled me forward. The pain of this hate and anger was like a fire inside of me. It was either going to consume or catapult me out of this situation. (It often catapulted me, but as you have seen, there were times when indeed it did consume me.) I hated the quality of my life so much that I was desperate to get out. If I hated being me, I had to change myself. It was the belief that I could change my life—that I *had* to change my life—that kept me dreaming. Dreaming of a better life gave me a reason to get up every day and do what was required or expected.

* * *

If you find yourself in a situation or life event where there seems to be hatred, opposition around you, or if you are basking in your own self-hatred, unable to feel you are loving, lovable, or that your life counts, there is always a way to change that belief, that feeling, that place of pain.

God placed you here on earth for a purpose. That purpose is not for you to hate yourself. It does not matter if other people through their ignorance have spoken unkind words to you. It does not matter if other people have not accepted you, if they have laughed at you or fired you. It does not matter if you were told you were unlovable, deserving hatred, or deserving little. What matters is if you believe them and what they say; but even if you do believe them, it is only a belief, and you can change that belief.

In order to overcome your obstacles and challenges and move from where you are to a place of love, peace, and power, you have to uproot the weeds of self-hatred. If others have done you wrong, if you have received an unfair predicament, if you have had people hurt you on purpose, lie to you, steal from you, try to rob you of peace of mind and even a reason to live, *stop. Pause.* There is a way for you to change. You are worthy of being loved.

Start by loving you. Affirm that you are worth loving. Affirm that you are not your past and that your future is going to be great. Look for other people to support you. They are out there: those who will affirm you, affirm your brightness in the world, even when you do not see it.

Life can and will change for you, but you have to work to overcome and challenge those old beliefs. Life can be better. I can attest to it. I recognized that doing something about my life was my responsibility no matter how deeply embedded or earnestly acquired my belief. Something on the inside buried deep within me propelled me to go one more day. I did not want to accept that the life that I had was the only life that I could lead. I did not want to passively accept my situation as it was.

In order to overcome any obstacle, one has to get in touch with their most authentic self—the real you. Listen to the voice within even when the water is rising around you and you have no boat and cannot swim. You can die in the hatred, or you can fight for your life. *Fight for your life!* The saying "Don't quit before your miracle comes" is true. Do not give up on yourself.

Find ways to get support if you are struggling for self-acceptance. Align yourself with people who see your worth. Align yourself with people who will support your cause—people who will love you in weakness and in strength. Some people have to deal with their life issues in therapy. Some do so by attending a church, some by following other positive people. Whatever it takes—do it! Don't pass up a chance for self-improvement.

One powerful tool is forgiveness; you can forgive yourself for not loving you. Forgiving the past will heal the past. Tell yourself that you love and accept you—all of you. Say it until you believe it and it will become you.

Forgive others for being so blind as to not recognize the greatness in you. Listen to your voice deep inside of you, the voice that God placed inside of you. Believe that you are born for wonderful things, no matter what others may say—because you are.

Just not hating myself opened up the door for so many other good things in my life. I have a life that is validating, I love myself, and I am at peace with myself and my past. I spend my time fulfilling my life purpose, which is to pass along the lessons and support those seeking a better way to be. I lived a large part of my life in self-hatred; moving from that place to a place of self-love and self-acceptance is better.

Not liking myself had kept me from being able to be open and receptive to others—even people who wanted to help me and wanted to support me. Now I'm free to openly share my triumphs and my failures and by doing so assist others on their life paths. There are so many people that can benefit from your story as well, of how you have overcome an obstacle, a challenge, and hate. Share your stories so that others may benefit. It will fill your life with hope for a better day and a better future, and it will help remind you just how much you matter when your days of challenge or setback come. Be kind to yourself. We all have challenges.

My new creed is this:

If I fail, I will still love me.
If I cannot fit into the clothes I once did, I will still love me.
If my relationship ends, I will still love me.
If someone hates me or speaks hate to me, I will still love me.
I will never give up on me or the dreams that help me wake
    up in the morning with a song.
I will never give up on me and the person God created me to be.
I will never lose hope.

Some days, moving forward may seem small. The earth can quake, but believe in yourself. Never allow the weeds to grow up and blind your vision for who you are and who God created you to be. You are worth loving.

No matter what you have been through, what you have done, or what others have done to you, it is possible to love yourself. God is love. God loves you. The Bible says love your neighbor as yourself. You have to love yourself first before you can love others and be authentically effective in life. Be determined and settled in your mind that you will live your life from a place of love—loving you, loving others, and loving what you do in your life.

CHAPTER 4

Wake Up Your Courageous Self

Is there anything or anyone that is intimidating you today or trying awfully hard to do so? What I mean is, are there people, circumstances, or even the voices in your head that are making you timid or downright fearful, so much so that you desire to retreat, stay small, or give up?

Maybe you work or live with someone who intimidates you. Around them, you feel like you don't have a voice or that what you offer isn't valuable. Maybe you fear that if you don't do what they want, you are at risk of danger, which causes you to dread some unknown consequence. Maybe there are areas of your life where you have hindered yourself through self-doubt or fear. Many times we say that we can do anything or live through anything except for. . . . What is your life exception?

* * *

As a child, I was intimidated daily.

Living in a tough neighborhood with a single mom who was on welfare, I was often scared. I rarely felt well cared for or protected, especially against the bullies.

We had big trees in the neighborhood, and in the summer, caterpillars would fall from the trees or the boys would climb up to get them. With a fistful of these creepy crawlers, the boys would grab the girls and stick the furry insects down our shirts, shove them in our hair, and laugh as we hysterically screamed, "Stop! Stop!" Frantically, we tried swiping them off us and we tried to get away.

Summer after summer this would happen; there was no let up. To try to get them to stop, we would do anything to get the things off us and just get away. Using our fear, these boys would demand that we give up the little candy money we had, make us go to the store and buy them things, and have us sweep their backyards; we were treated like slaves. And we did everything they asked—anything to avoid having caterpillars crawling down our backs. Eventually, they merely had to use the word *caterpillar* and that would be enough to intimidate us and cause us to do whatever they wanted.

One day, I had had enough and I made a decision. I don't know where this came from, but I decided I wasn't having this anymore. No matter how much I hated to have the caterpillars put down my back, I was not going to run anymore. I was no longer going to give these boys the satisfaction of watching me squeal, run away, or do what they wanted. It was one of the first moments in my life where I realized that I had power and I was done giving it to them.

That day I was shaking so much on the inside it was like being in the midst of a 10.0 earthquake. Intention is one thing; action is another! I announced to the caterpillar terrorists, "I am not running. I am not afraid of the caterpillars. I can hold them and have them all over me. I am *not* running."

The lesson of my stand against the caterpillars, which has been reinforced regularly throughout my life, is that I do not have to run from my fear. I haven't always won in that battle. As you have read, I have often succumbed to it and tried to escape. But over and over I would be reminded of the caterpillar wars, and I would delight at the memory of the confusion and shock in the eyes of those big, bad boys when I refused to play their game.

Now, just because you say "no" once does not mean the problem goes away. You must keep standing your ground. These bullies tried me a few more times, but I didn't back down. Those moments of courage, those moments of calling my own power forth, changed things for me and for them. It wasn't long before they no longer bothered me.

And, it turns out, courage is contagious. The other girls now looked up to me, and some of them gained enough courage to challenge their bullies and meet their fears. When they did, they no longer had to go through this year after year.

* * *

You, too, can acknowledge that "I am afraid of this thing" but then decide that you want to be on the other side of it all. You, too, can say, "I want to conquer this fear." Perhaps you are dealing with your own creepy caterpillars, and like me, you have no one to protect you or make them stop. Maybe the voices in your head are threatening you in some way, causing you to fear stepping out or taking a stand. We can feel quite powerless, alone, and forced to do as we are told, or else.

That's OK. I had allowed the caterpillars to be placed on my arm, back, or anywhere that the boys wanted to throw them, and my first step to escape that was to take control of what I could—my reaction. I had no way of knowing what would happen, but I survived it. I was willing to take the risk. My self-respect was worth it.

You, too, have to confront your fears. Who criticizes you? Who is telling you, "You do not have what it takes to make it"? Don't give others the power over you. Embodying someone else's thoughts or opinions of you can and will limit your vision of your life. It will keep the bullies laughing at you and make you run from a life of self-worth and self-acceptance. It can keep you from having your smallest or largest dream actualized.

You deserve to have your dreams, to be able to reach out and accomplish your goals, to walk in your greatest desire and see its fulfillment. Don't allow the voice of your fear to tell you that you are too weak, lacking education, or lacking in the confidence you need to succeed. Don't allow your fears to tell you that it is too late or that you are too old to achieve your dreams. Don't allow the fear of being judged or criticized by others stop you.

When I decided to tell my story, some of my old fears came to visit. I had to say to the voices, "OK, thank you for sharing, but I have a story that is worth telling. I have been through so many obstacles and I know there are other people who feel the same way. My story is important to tell. My passion to help others is bigger than the fear of not being good enough." I had to tap into my courageous self and set the record straight!

How I chose to act at the time of them grabbing me and putting caterpillars down my top was a moment of transformation for me. Just as a caterpillar transforms into a butterfly, I transformed from afraid to fearsome. No longer was the caterpillar a symbol of shame and intimidation but one of respect and power.

My desire to see other people rise up to the majesty of their life is all-consuming. I want to see others rise to a place where they can believe in themselves regardless of their fears, regardless of their failures, and have a fulfilling life. I know it can be done because I am doing it.

You have a courageous self within you, too. Stand up and be accounted for. Your choice can bring transformation to you and to others watching you. Your life does matter. Your visions and dreams do matter.

Of course, I do not propose that you take an action that would compromise your safety—facing down a wild animal or encouraging a violent domestic relationship. To stand and let the bear attack or to let another individual cause physical or emotional bodily harm to you is not what I am proposing. Run and get help in these situations. But just making a decision that you are not going to allow your fears to stop you means you are well on your way to face whatever it is that challenges you, whatever it is that you fear.

This will quiet your mind and help you act calmly. Speak words of courage and affirm that you can do something even when you are shaking on the inside.

I once read that the process going on within the cocoon, which transforms a caterpillar into a butterfly, is truly amazing. Once wrapped up tightly, the caterpillar literally melts down into a liquid, during which time they only retain the starting points for their most important features, including the eyes and wings.

There is a butterfly inside of you waiting to grow wings and fly. You may be encountering some challenges right now, and you may not see wings or the means to overcome. But be determined to not allow others to scare, stop, or crush your spirit. Stand your ground. By doing so, you are standing up for yourself. You can overcome your fears, develop your wings, meet the challenge, and became a hero to others who also have the same fears.

If you have to melt down to a liquid, retaining only the drive and vision inside your heart and soul, do so! Be your courageous self, and your wings will surely come.

CHAPTER 5

Your Desires Matter

Does it appear that your desires, dreams, and goals are all going unfulfilled? Do you feel as though you have struggled and have nothing to show for the dreams that are in your heart? Have you been told that "those silly thoughts do not matter" or "you can never have what you want"? Or have you been told that you are too old, too dumb, not smart enough, not tall enough, not rich enough, not pretty enough, or not strong enough, or that you don't know the right people?

Well, I am here to tell you that your desires do matter; the dreams you have envisioned for your life matter. Do you feel like you want to give up on your dreams because after all this time, you have not seen any fulfillment? Perhaps other people have moved on and achieved their goals and you are still waiting? Perhaps, also, you have not seen a rainbow of hope or a signpost that says, "You are on your way. Keep at it." Well, I want to encourage you to keep at it.

* * *

As a child, I often had strong desires, but my desires seemed impossible—I was a kid and what I wanted usually required money, something that we were always short on.

One of those burning desires was to become a Girl Scout. However, my mother did not have the funds for me to join, which included the registration and a uniform. My mother's eyes said it all: "Girl, I ain't interested in your little Girl Scout thing." When I pressed on in spite of her reaction, she said, "I do not have any money for that. I done told you don't bother me with that stuff." The spark in my eyes dimmed momentarily, but I did not give up.

I would see the Girl Scouts in their uniforms at my church, and twice a year, there was a parade. I would spot the Girl Scouts marching down the street. Oh, how I wanted that to be me, marching down the street in our neighborhood and all the way downtown in my Girl Scout uniform! I wanted to be the Girl Scout who lived out the creed to do good to others, to help others, to honor the Girl Scout way. But how could I make this happen?

An entire year passed since my initial petition to my mother, and I found a way! I met a lady who wanted someone to walk her son to and from school, watch him until she came home, and tutor him. I did well in my position, and before long, I had a few more customers. I soon earned enough money to pay my own way into the Girl Scout troupe! This was better than Santa Claus—better than the toys under a Christmas tree! At that time, it was better than anything because I was now going to realize my dream, and I had made it happen by myself.

I went to church one Sunday and inquired about when the Girl Scout troupe met and was given the information. I showed up at the next meeting, my funds in hand, my heart singing. I became a Girl Scout! I was a full-fledged, handbook-carrying, uniform-wearing Girl Scout! My dream came true, and I had made it happen.

* * *

Maybe you desire a better job, an education, a dream to come true, a relationship, a membership to a club, a seminar you have wanted to take but did not know how you could enroll or pay for it.

What you desire can happen for you just as it happened for me. Think about it: I was a kid, living in the ghetto, told that I could not do it and that there were no funds. A year passed by, and I nurtured my desire to become a Girl Scout. The vision of marching in a parade flamed inside of me and ignited my desire to join. And, by the way, I marched in the annual parade proudly in my uniform. I also received several badges for completing advanced requirements; they were elective, but I wanted them all.

Don't give up. If you really desire something, there is always some way to achieve what you want, if you really want it. Your desire could be right around the corner, even in your backyard. It may not look exactly like you thought it would and therefore may be harder to recognize. Just keep doing something to move it forward.

* * *

I had a friend, Katy, who came from a family with nineteen kids. Although Katy was older than me, we still became friends. Her sister, Dede, was around my age but one grade below me in school. She hated me! I am not sure why, but she did. She would taunt me whenever I was over at her house to see Katy. If she was not taunting me, I received the silent treatment.

One day when I went to her house to hang out with her sister, she was on her way out the door, but to my surprise, she spoke politely to me. My mouth flew open and I could barely, faintly squeak out, "Hi Dee." I did not know what had changed her behavior, but I wanted some of that!

Katy told me that they had all been baptized and joined their family church. She invited me to go with them the next Sunday. Well, let me tell you, I went to that church, and it was an explosion of great music, sweet- and melodic-sounding voices, clapping of hands, and a preacher who spoke loudly and powerfully. I loved being there. Everyone was warm and inviting. They were not focused on their big hats, great looking shoes, or expensive clothes. They spoke of God and love, and I wanted to be a part of that place.

The following Sunday I went again and joined the church. However, when my mother found out, she was not happy. I don't know why, but she did not want me going to that church and would not allow me to attend. I wanted nothing more in the whole wide world than to go there. I saw a major transformation happen there. I knew I should be there. The presence of God was there. It was loving, healing, and life giving. There were hugs—something I never got growing up. This was a place of love. I knew it!

My mother made me stop going. I was no longer allowed to leave home and attend that church, and I did not want to go to her church. So rather than give up, I decided I would have church in our backyard. I was eleven or twelve, and when my friends and I would hang out, I said, "Hey, let's have church out here. Y'all could sing and I will speak."

Our little services became a weekly thing, and lots of people from the neighborhood would come. (Only God gets the glory for that.) Words of life and encouragement would flow from my mouth. I later learned that this was the anointing of God flowing out of me to help, bless, and encourage others. I would read and study the Bible and speak from my heart what I believed was important for our spiritual growth and development. I was being an instrument, a voice to help others who needed a word of encouragement or a message of hope. Young people and adults alike would come to our little service. Some parents told their children to be a part of our little weekly backyard gathering.

That summer, God brought hope to our little neighborhood through singing, praising, teaching, and believing what His word promised. We did not know much, but we were all hungry for something positive in the midst of our crime-infested neighborhood. And we found it. We had a great, joyful summer by taking church to our backyard.

* * *

Often getting the things I desired as a child seemed impossible. Many obstacles stood in my way. But what you want is often right there, waiting for you to discover.

Some of you are hungry for a word of hope, a signpost to let you know you are on the right track. If you are reading this book, I do not believe you are reading it by chance or a lucky draw. You are reading this book because God wants you to listen to His voice—the voice that says you can make it, you can have hope and have a good future.

I was reading in Psalms 103 one day when I was feeling particularly vulnerable and saw the scripture that says God knows our frame. Wow. He knows me. He knows those little weak and fragile places inside of me. He sends His word, another person, a book, a podcast to you to encourage you. He knows what is inside of you and what you need and what needs to come out—greatness that wants to come out, a part that needs healing, a part of you that wants to reach to others and help them heal. It is all inside of you.

* * *

When I was in graduate school, I met a lady from Dallas. We became good friends. She once told me some of her life story, which included that she had had seven abortions. She said that she had been careless and became pregnant eight times. The first time she became pregnant she was a young teenage girl, and she gave birth. She gave that child up for adoption.

Initially I was shocked by her candidness, but I knew her to be a very loving person. She was afraid to have the stigma and shame of that first pregnancy revisit her, and so she hid all of her pregnancies through abortion. One of her abortions was considered illegal, and she nearly bled to death. (This is not judgment about the rightness or wrongness of abortion.)

She was a good friend to me. After college, we kept in touch. She became a well-known professor in a small southern town and married a wonderful man who was also a professor. He wanted a child, but she felt unworthy of another pregnancy. Deep down inside of her, she really did want to be a mother.

After trying for a long time, she discovered that she was now unable to give birth to a child. She was depressed, her biological clock was running out, but she did not want to disappoint her husband.

She and I would talk weekly, and I encouraged her to forgive herself and maybe look into adopting a child. It took a while for her to come around, but she and her husband finally agreed to adopt, and they adopted a newborn baby. She was so happy. She said that adoption was a great thing. Someone adopted her baby when she was a thirteen-year-old teenager, and now she had adopted a baby.

She had often cried clandestinely thinking that being a mother was the one dream she would never realize, but she finally did it!

* * *

Your desire matters. It is not important how long you have held on to the desire; if it is alive and burning inside of you, revisit it. Honor it. You deserve to achieve and reach those desires that you are passionate about, those desires that were aborted because they seemed unthinkable. Those desires want to live again inside of you. Let them live. Do not let anyone discourage you, including yourself.

Inside an oyster is a beautiful pearl, but it develops by building layer upon layer. When it emerges as a shining pearl, all the work has been done. All that you need to do is begin to put down your layers. Keep believing or start believing again in yourself and your desires. God does not hold anything against us. We might hold things against others and other people might too, but not God. He wants you to have the desires of your heart. The grain of sand is already there; your pearl is waiting to come out.

Not everything is achievable in a strictly translated form—I can't fly like a bird (but I can take a plane); I am 5'3" and will never be 5'6" (but I can wear higher shoes). Be open to multiple ways in which you achieve your goals—more education, a new job, a better job, financial independence, owning your own company, having a baby, or hosting a church in your backyard. You can always find a way to achieve them. There is always a way for you to change.

CHAPTER 6

Get Up, Get Away, Get Going

Sometimes no matter how hard you try in a given environment, the circumstances, the people who surround you, and the general atmosphere can have such a strong gravitational pull downward that eventually you just can't stand any longer. This was the case for me. I became aware that in order to make positives changes for myself, I had to get out of my poverty-stricken life. I had to get away. In order for me to change, I could not remain in the same place doing the same things.

Sometimes the best thing you can do is change your environment.

* * *

Despite the fact that we couldn't escape to the low-income housing project that had seemed like salvation, I continued to hold the dream of a different and better life. I was certain that I did not want to live my life with "less than"—never experiencing the richer, fuller life that I so desired.

I wanted a real bathroom with a bathtub and hot running water, a bed that was free of bedbugs, a place to lie down and gaze up without having to cover my face from the roaches dropping from the ceiling onto my bed. The roaches were everywhere—on the floor, inside the cabinets, inside the refrigerator (yes, those were some hungry roaches), and on the walls and ceiling.

But I didn't just want a more comfortable environment; I was desperately in need of some validation of who I was. The final push to propel me out of the life I did not want was rejection from the one place that really mattered to me—my church.

In high school I was the president of the young people's group at church (birth to thirty). As part of my position, I would visit other churches when they had special meetings for young people, and I was usually asked to speak. My friends told me that I had put our church (a small storefront church) on the map. I would invite people to attend our special Sunday afternoon programs where choirs would perform and we would have a guest minister. I interacted with many churches and was often a guest speaker for them. God had truly blessed me. I was able to call on the most well-known bishop in St. Louis, ask him to come and speak at our program, and he would come. People from churches all around knew my name. I was a diligent and faithful young girl, sincerely worshiping God.

My life was so fulfilled! And then suddenly it all went away—quickly and permanently away. I was the victim of sexual abuse by a church member. When I sought some intervention from the church—someone who could help me, I was called a liar. Rumors flew quickly, and the retaliation was swift and painful! The pastor's wife had me publically silenced in church for six months. I could not participate in my beloved youth group. The entire congregation believed that I was a bad girl, a backslider.

I was rejected by my church, the place that meant the most to me, and given the silent treatment. This rejection hit me beyond my level of endurance. I feared that if I did not leave town, I might succumb to *being* a bad girl and prove them right—that I was a backslider on my way to great destruction. I couldn't bear that.

What a sentence to place on a child, young adult, or anyone really. Through their treatment of me, I came to believe that God was mad at me. I later, of course, learned this was not true. His plans and purpose were neither to hurt nor kill me but rather that I would have life and have it more abundantly.

My job was to figure out *how* to get away. I finally decided that my ticket out of poverty and mistreatment and into a better way of living would be through academia. Once my path became clear, I set about in earnest to take the actions that would get me there. I worked very hard to make it into a good college—one that was far away from the place that had shaped, scarred, and scared me—and a safer environment for myself.

The first step was to study diligently. I sought out every opportunity to do well in school. I dreamed of actual colleges and read their catalogs, imaging what life there might be like.

The next step was a bit hard for me—I had some trust issues at this point. I needed to find others to support me and help me in my plan. It was too big for just me to handle. It's amazing what resources you can find once you open your eyes and look for them. Fortunately, I found people in my life who were very encouraging to me.

One such person was a kind teacher named Mrs. Fennoy. I loved that lady. Not only was she proud of me, but she also provided a job, hope, and self-respect. She let me clean her house on Saturdays for two years while I was in high school.

This grand privilege afforded me some independence, the ability to buy toiletries, transportation (a weekly bus pass), and some of the things that those who came from better-off homes took for granted. Every Saturday, after working, she would treat me to a good meal along with positive words of encouragement. It gave me a window into another world to which I aspired, and she believed I could get there.

There were others, too. I had some distant relatives who were educated, and they heartily approved of my decision. Instrumental to my getting into college was my high school counselor. In his own way, he inspired me and pushed me forward. He provided applications for college, which included writing an autobiographical essay. After I had completed all the required testing, applications, and essays, he directly assisted me and other students in obtaining scholarships.

And I did get a scholarship—to one of the esteemed Ivy League colleges, Cornell University! My dream and desire to get out came true.

Of course, that doesn't mean that the obstacles went away. One last major hurdle was the actual physical break from my life. Getting away and going to school was bittersweet. My mother disapproved greatly. For me to leave and go to college meant she would be receiving less money from welfare, which would leave her in a strain financially, as she could barely pay the monthly rent as it was. That hurt me; I felt bad. Yet I knew I could not help her or me by remaining where I was. So off I went!

At college, I knew that I had a chance for a new beginning—no one knew me or anything about my past. It was a clean slate; I could totally reinvent myself. I had nothing to lose. Everyone there was excited about being in college. There was a positive atmosphere, focus, and excitement in the air; it was a fertile place to make changes. I decided I would go to the library daily for study and would learn a new word each day. I would walk tall with my confidence high and project that I was a powerful, smart, and independent person.

Guess what? That is what everyone else saw in me. Ah! I had painted a picture of me with a different future—a future planned and orchestrated by the vision of what I wanted to become. And now I began mimicking others who appeared that way as well.

* * *

We all need to be in a place where we can feel safe, a place where we can stretch, learn, grow, and make mistakes without feeling that our safety is compromised. We all do best when we do not feel that our creativity, hopes, and dreams are being compromised, thwarted, or sabotaged.

You can create a different story for your life instead of living out the one written by someone else for you. I grew up in poverty as a child, but I did not write that story. I needed to rewrite the one that had been projected on me. College gave me a chance to create a different theme than the one written in my childhood environment—live in poverty and die in poverty. You, too, can rewrite your stories by making changes from the way things are to the dream that you have for your life. Getting away may help you live out a new story for yourself without the constraints of all your old beliefs and mind-sets.

I knew that if I changed my environment, I would feel better about myself; reinventing myself was possible. The new people I would meet were in the self-improvement business (getting an education is really about self-improvement), and I would have acceptance from others.

I would have an opportunity to be around people who would validate me and would want what I want in life. Changing your environment will help you find people you want to be like, and it helps you create that vision for yourself.

In order to make some critical changes in your life, you may need to change your location, your environment, or just stop hanging out with your present crowd and find people who are in the process of obtaining something that you want or something similar to what you want or who have already achieved a level of success that is in line with your goals and vision.

For me, change meant that as I was rewriting my future and increasing the voices of hope inside of me. The voices that had said "I will never make it" changed to "I can make it." I let go of the prewritten, prepackaged future that my old environment, the assignment from childhood, held for me.

But in order for me to change, I had to hate what I had. Not dislike it—hate it. I hated my life in poverty. I hated the sickness of hopelessness. There was something inside of me, my inner spirit, pushing me for more. I think we all have it. We just have to listen to our own voices, the ones that tell us where we want to go—places of safety, self-acceptance, wealth, and an environment that reflects our inner magnificence.

Each of us must find our own motivation for change. It may be a longtime yearning or a sudden event that causes one to want to move from their pain to a place of peace and power.

Getting away to college may not be your answer for changing your life; however, educating yourself for something that stretches you is always a start. This could be finishing a degree or obtaining some skills that will help place you at your next level of success.

A client of mine went back to school at age fifty-two to obtain her GED and then went on to a private and expensive nursing school. She now works as a licensed practical nurse. It was difficult but obtainable. She loves it. It was a dream she had long held, but she never felt she could measure up to it or pass all the math and science classes that were required.

I encouraged her to look at what was next on her list of things that she wanted to accomplish in life. On her new list, she wanted to open a home for women who are homeless, women who experience many bumps along their roads in life, such as divorce, unemployment, or recovery from drug addiction. She wanted to work with women who are willing to change their perception of who they are by giving them a new environment while they work on some of the issues and mind-sets that led them there. She wanted to help them change their mind-sets and visualize the life they want to live.

To do this, she had to move from her beautiful home. She made many sacrifices and waned in and out of encouragement. She is now living her dream and inspiring others as well.

What is next for you? Take a moment, let go of all the obstacles in your way, and just see yourself living out your dream and your heart's desire. What does that look like? What will motivate you? What must you do to make it happen? What is the cost? How will you start your new journey? Write all of this down; that's how a dream becomes a plan.

I wish that all my changes could have come by wishing and hoping, but that is not the way it works. Reading books; enrolling in seminars; watching videos; enrolling in mastermind groups, self-help groups, or groups that promote making positive changes that will help you to create the life you long to have are good positive actions that you can take. Every change requires some action.

Being rich or wealthy is unknown to someone facing extreme poverty, and moving from where you are to where you want to be is only doable when you stop the old video and silence the voices telling you that you cannot achieve your goals—the voices that have been spinning around in your head from your childhood. They may even be new voices that do not validate you; say you have attempted to do something but did not succeed. You may have failed a test, flunked out of school, been fired on a job. You may have been told that you did not make the cut, or you may have had a bad relationship. It does not mean you are a failure. It means you may need to change your direction. Sometimes just leaving your locality and relocating to a new place can help revitalize your vision for your life. For certain, you must address the voices that tell you that you do not matter.

One of the ways to stop the negative voices of others is to speak to them and disagree with them. If your environment is full of hopeless voices or people who have lost faith in their own hopes and dreams, you may need to leave them. Getting away means getting out of town or getting away from the places, people, and situations that are shaping or keeping you in a holding pattern in your life.

Don't forget to look for those who will support you in your process; look for those with affirming and encouraging voices. Look for individuals that can serve as a resource for you in your journey. Don't be afraid to invest in your self-growth through a personal coach or mentor, seminars, or places like mastermind groups. There will always be those positioned by God to help you along your journey. They are there and will appear. But you must take action. They will probably not come to your house and knock on your door.

You can change. God, in His magnificence, made us that way. He says, "Seek and you shall find. Knock and the door will open. Ask and it shall be given to you." You are reading this book not by accident but by divine appointment. You are where you should be to begin your new life. It can happen for you and it will. Don't give up on you. Do not let anyone or any situation define how far you want to go in life. Think big. Dream big.

Learning how to find the best path for your life begins with the desire that you want to make changes. You then must follow through with action. Starting over can have a big impact on your success. Reinvent yourself; rescript your future. Change your environment; if you cannot make a geographical change, then change the messages in your mind. Change the voices you are listening to—yours and the voices of others. Renounce the voices of defeat.

Your best days are ahead; don't let moments of setback stop you. You may have been trying to make changes, but they seem elusive or not lasting. *Keep going!*

Now is your time. It is your time to walk in the majesty that God created in you and for you. Get up, get away, and get into action.

CHAPTER 7

You Can Overcome Any Addiction

I wanted to quit, but I loved the fix.

When we are trying to find a vision (dream, voice, high calling) inside of us, we often fail to recognize it, or we direct it instead of discovering it—which does not create an authentic result. We do things to anesthetize our failure to accomplish what we want and to live out who we truly are.

Drugs are a great distractor, a great deceiver. One can be grand and on top of the world without ever leaving a bed or couch. Drugs are an equal-opportunity employer. One can spend hundreds of thousands of dollars to be an employee. One can turn over the weekly paycheck to drugs. It is OK whatever the arrangement is; in the end, drugs win.

* * *

I was deceived and became an employee of *Use Drugs to Hide from Your Life, Inc.*

I went through a period of drug use and experimentation, and I stayed longer than I should have. I paid more than what I had, using drugs for pleasure, for partying, for days of being on top of the world, being creative, days of depression, days of joy, and nights of sadness.

When I was a teenager, I attended a church that believed in praying for the sick, and the faithful were taught openly to take no medicine. There were people taking medication, and I do not remember any radical sanctions from the pulpit if someone did take it. However, many in the congregation did adhere to the teaching of relying on prayer rather than medicine.

Being very devout, I did not take medication for most ailments, including headaches, stomach cramps, or colds. I also remembered reading something in the Bible about strong drinks being bad. I decided that what it referred to was soda. I do not remember consuming sodas much after the age of thirteen. We were pretty poor, so soda had never really been on my snack list.

At that time, using drugs or taking medication was unthinkable! That would never be me.

During college when I did occasionally start drinking soda again, I would mix water with the soda, as it was too strong for me to drink without diluting it. My friends thought I was a bit of an oddity, so it seemed like just another quirk.

In my early college years, I did not drink alcohol. Anything that altered my consciousness was avoided at all costs. I felt that I needed to be in control at all times. I was fearful of someone taking advantage of me—a flashback to my unsafe feelings as a child and the episodes of sexual abuse. Self-protection was very important to me, and I would keep a watchful vigil at all times. My blouses were buttoned up to the top, as I did not believe in showing any skin. Being covered from head to toe made me feel protected.

But while I was in college, I did eventually experiment with drugs. Several people I knew smoked marijuana, and while I was not a smoker because of asthma, I would indulge when I was around friends who smoked.

When I moved to Los Angeles, I worked for a record company, and I was introduced to people who worked in the business and who used drugs frequently and were willing to share. This is where I met the self that I did not know existed. This was the self that thought I was OK, but the pain from my past came to visit me in various ways.

Los Angeles is a great place to live. It is glamorous and exciting, especially when one is working in and or around the entertainment business.

Little by little, I became an occasional user of recreational drugs. I would go periods without using and then return to the drugs. Eventually, drugs became a common part of my life, just as common as getting up and taking a shower. When things were good, I would use, and when things were bad, I would use.

In spite of a good job, I was never able to catch up with my bills or manage my life. No matter what I did to get ahead, I was living in small apartments, driving a car without air or heat. For some reason, I just could not afford my life, and I just never seemed to measure up. While other friends were being successful, I was not.

Was something wrong with my DNA? I just knew nothing fit. I was not present in my life, and certainly I could not say that I was taking good care of myself. I was always a day away from eviction or being fired.

It did not look like it to some, but I *was* lost. I was hurting—being smart but living dumb. There was so much loneliness, so much pain of not feeling that I was enough. The dots would just not connect. I needed a new direction for my life.

Drugs became my new best friend—a friend that did not disapprove of me, a friend that would make me feel better about myself. In the end, my friend turned on me and became cunning, baffling, and powerful—it was a very strong hold. I was a slave to its power for too long.

I did not look like an addict for the most part, but when I was alone with my drugs, I knew the truth. I read an article in *Time* magazine about cocaine—the evil empire. I had not been able to put it in words, but it was true. It is an empire of addiction, an empire of evil, because no one comes out better as a result of using drugs.

I was tired of wanting one more high, looking for one more hit, finding a stash that I had forgotten I had hidden. I was able to slow down my using on many occasions, but as the days went by, I would return to my friend. My life became unmanageable.

In desperation, I tried therapy and spent thousands of dollars on a therapist who turned out to be a user of cocaine and marijuana! She was not a healthy therapist and frequently played with my emotions. When she was sober, she felt I should try a program of recovery. When she would slip, she would confess her indiscretions. She said that I reminded her of herself. My friends all hated my therapist and begged me to stop going to her. But I was addicted to her illness and the cat and mouse game that she played with me. Her therapist had committed suicide, and I had attempted suicide many times. She was fascinated with that and admitted that she had often wanted to commit suicide as well. She even invited me to her home in the Pacific Palisades. I was crazy; she was crazy. In many ways, this sick individual validated my existence—the one that kept me addicted.

However, one good thing came from knowing her, and that was my introduction to the twelve-step program. By attending meetings, I met the most wonderful woman, and she became my sponsor. She accepted me—messed up, crazy, and all. She was a mentor and friend, and she understood my loneliness. She would invite me to her family dinners for Thanksgiving and Christmas holidays, the major holidays when people tend to feel the loneliest. She was an amazing woman—a pillar of hope and strength. I am so grateful for that divine connection. I will always love her.

Attending the twelve-step program helped me regain a part of my life. It did not, however, arrest the desire to harm myself through suicide. I did land in the hospital for attempted suicide once after my recovery from drugs.

There was also one accidental drug overdose partly due to incorrect medical advice. Sick with asthma and respiratory problems, following several trips to the emergency room, I received the wrong medication and slipped into a coma. But that trip to the hospital delivered the final piece of what I needed to truly regain the life I wanted.

After I came out of the coma, I had a respiratory therapist who would come and give me breathing treatments twice a day. She was cheerful, upbeat, and appeared genuinely concerned about the patients she served. She was a Christian and not ashamed to say so. She became a big sister to me spiritually. She was one more person that God placed in my life to support me and not criticize me. Through God's unmerited, unearned grace and favor on my life, I survived this dark period.

Today, I am clean from all illegal drugs. I have sobriety of mind and heart.

* * *

There is help for anyone who is suffering from drugs or alcohol or other addictions. I made a choice to use drugs to anesthetize my pain and disappointments. If you are actively using or had sobriety and lost it, there is hope and help. Alcoholic Anonymous is available worldwide. There are other programs for people, depending on what works for them. These programs are all free. I have included a resource list in Appendix B to help you get started. There are also many paid programs to help with addiction. Some people do not like the twelve-step programs because the word God is used. Many people use the term *higher power*. There are also programs for people who do not want to use the term *God* or *higher power*.

Do whatever it takes to get yourself clean and sober. You owe that to yourself and those who love you.

CHAPTER 8

Conquering Breast Cancer

I am a survivor of breast cancer twice over. However, I hesitated to include this part of my struggle because cancer is so prevalent today and almost everyone alive has been touched by someone they know who has or has survived cancer. But I think it is important to recognize that the unexpected may occur, and it's important to understand how to manage this type of occurrence in your life as well. Thank God for all the research out there and for all the supportive groups that are available. I think *support* is the most important word when dealing with this life obstacle.

* * *

The "C" word came to me as a message from a phone call. "There is something wrong with the film from the mammogram that you had last week and we'd like you to come back in and retake it right away." Immediately, I knew something was wrong. Two weeks prior to this phone call, I had gone to the doctor because I was not feeling well. I was having some breast pain, and I asked if perhaps I should have a mammogram. The doctor told me I was probably just getting too much caffeine and advised me to eliminate it from my diet. I did not fall within the guidelines for having a baseline mammogram—I was too young and did not have a strong family history of cancer. I insisted that I wanted one, and he eventually relented with a flourish, "It will just be a waste of time."

A week later, I received a letter in the mail stating that my film was normal. I felt so relieved. It was probably just the caffeine, and I immediately went cold turkey on it.

The following week, however, I received a call from the radiology department asking me to return immediately for another mammogram—there was something on the first film. I returned for a second mammogram.

The radiology technician delivered those fateful words, "There it is." I had a mass on my breast. The first film had been misread. It was only when the radiologist discovered that my film had not yet been filed that the issue was spotted. The radiologist asked the technician if I had been informed of the positive reading, and they confronted the discrepancy from there.

I definitely had cancer. They told me that an appointment with a surgeon was scheduled for that day. The surgeon set up a biopsy and informed me that if it was positive, they would remove the cancer.

I was out of my mind—crazy and tearful! Cancer? Cancer! What would this mean—surgery and most likely treatments? How could this happen to me? What was wrong with me? Was I going to be OK? I lived alone and had no close family living near me. Could all this be true?

The biopsy confirmed that indeed I had a mass and it was a carcinoma. I was numb. My surgeon suggested a radical mastectomy on my left breast and most likely adjuvant therapy with radiation and chemotherapy. I did not want my breast removed. When I asked the doctor what would he tell his wife to do if she had breast cancer, he told me that he would recommend lumpectomy and adjuvant therapy, radiation, and most likely chemotherapy. He said, however, that removal of the breast with follow-up treatment was the standard practice. I was still young and dating and could not wrap my mind around losing a breast. I went for a second opinion by a female surgeon at a different hospital who ran a breast clinic. She told me that I would not need to have my breast removed.

At the time of my diagnosis, I weighed about 105 pounds, exercised at least four times a week, and ate decent foods. So why cancer? Was there something defective inside of me? Was God punishing me? My doctor told me that it was like playing cards and that was the hand that was dealt to me. Aha! It was the only thing that made sense for me. I did not have to blame myself. It was the hand life had given me, and I would play it out.

When I told my family and friends about the cancer, they were all supportive. I had the surgery and treatment (but kept my breast). During that time, I realized that I had to be good to my body. It had felt as if my body betrayed me. I also felt that it was just another way to say, "I'm not good enough," the recurring theme in my life.

At the time of my diagnosis, I did not know anyone who had ever had cancer. I did not know anyone who knew anyone who had breast cancer. I had no idea how to even begin to find support for myself. It was really hard back then—no social media, not a lot of organizations for those with cancer. When I did find a group, it was far away and difficult to get to. Ultimately, I felt alone.

A particularly disheartening experience in my search for help was the discovery of a wonderful research study that had been done on breast cancer, only to find out that it did not include women of African American descent. It seemed another sign that I did not qualify for something.

Before I completed my treatments, I got a call from a friend who knew of someone who was newly diagnosed with cancer, and they asked me if I would talk to their friend—of course, I did. This happened several times, and I decided to form a support group of my own for women in the San Fernando Valley. I did not want anyone else to feel the loneliness that I had felt when I was diagnosed and going for treatments.

We met once a month for support, but I was always available for another sister who was diagnosed with cancer. I went with many of the women to the doctor, helped them get their medical records quickly, and went with them to their treatments. I bought groceries, found financial assistance for some, and negotiated donated time-off for a woman who had lost her medical benefits. This was the kind of help provided for women in my support group—Circle of Women. It also gives you some idea of the extensive amount of support that one person can need during this difficult time.

My first battle with cancer occurred in 1989. My second battle began in 2008. A routine mammogram looked suspicious; this time it was caught early and, although it was aggressive in morphology, I only underwent radiation treatments. I drove sixty miles to work every day and went to radiation treatments on my lunch break, returned to work, and then drove another sixty miles home. It was a big push, but I wanted my children to know that when things happen to us that are out of our control, we can still manage our lives and not give up. Today, I am fine and cancer free and so grateful to be alive.

* * *

When I first had breast cancer, I had to search to find out about support. People were still whispering the word cancer and or just not talking about it so much. My story is here to encourage anyone with cancer. You are not alone. There is an army of us out in the world, living our lives, stronger because we are now on the other side of cancer.

I've included my tips about coping with cancer in Appendix C to serve as resource for support. I no longer have a cancer support group; however, I continue to support women with cancer and am affiliated with a couple of large breast cancer organizations. Remember—breast cancer is a diagnosis, not a death sentence. Early detection is important.

My strategies for coping with cancer are as follows:

- Never give up.
- Get up, dress up, and show up.
- Allow yourself to grieve.
- Allow yourself to rest.
- Sleep all day if you need it. Your body is undergoing strange and unusual things.

- Chemotherapy is such a bad drug to have to take, but it can help prolong and save lives.
- Allow others to help you and do footwork for you.
- Believe in yourself.

Know that you are the expert when it comes to your body. Do not let a doctor define you and make all your decisions. It's just a job for them. It is your life—your body, your heart, mind, and soul. You do know the answers. If you feel that you cannot make the best decision, pray over it and have your spouse, a friend, a relative, or someone you trust who shares your vision of wellness help you. You will overcome.

CHAPTER 9

Change Your Script: Change Your Life

> A man shall be satisfied with the fruit of his mouth, and with the increase of his lips shall he be filled. Death and life are in the power of the tongue.
>
> —*Proverbs 18:21, KJV*

When I was growing up, my oldest brother would always say, "I will be like my dad [his dad died at age thirty-two], except I will die before I am thirty." He was an innocent boy who just said something that sounded cute and brave. He would be like his dad.

When he grew up, my brother spent four years in the Air Force. He was able to travel the world and was fluent in French and Italian. He received a degree from the University of Maryland and became very successful in his own business. He had a home, a wife, and two small children. Everything appeared to be going well for him, until one rainy night on a bridge.

My beloved brother was involved in a solo car accident. He had been happy and feeling good; no drugs or alcohol were involved. I do not know how long he had chanted that he would be dead before the age of thirty, but he died at age twenty-six.

His words—consistently spoken, chanted, and visualized—preceded the event. Flashbacks of our younger years together were screaming inside of my head: "I'll be dead before I am thirty." That was his script. I truly believe that killed him more than all the injuries he sustained.

* * *

Our words matter. Words in our head become words we say out loud. Words we say out loud become actions.

I was once working with a client who had been in a motorcycle accident. As a result, she had been awarded over two million dollars as a settlement. Now wealthy—a big change in her life—she said that her money isolated her and she was lonely.

She told me that she always used to say that she would be a millionaire by the time she was thirty-five and that she would probably be lonely as result because she would not know who she could trust. We talked about the power of words and worked on affirmations that would bring her friends and good relationships. We worked on rewriting her script to say that people loved being with her. Her new affirmation described how people valued her (as she valued them) and that friends add value to her life, just as her warmth and caring adds value to her friends.

We also worked on trust issues. She had not trusted people in her young life. She was surrounded by drugs and prostitution and was betrayed by many people whom she had trusted. Her solution at the time was to resolve that friends did not matter and that she would find a way to be self-sufficient, even wealthy.

As a result of our work together, she began carrying her affirmations in her wallet and made flash cards to serve as bookmarks. Eventually she had two to three good friends. It all came about because she changed her script. She worked on releasing and forgiving all the people in her past life who had disappointed her. She changed her script about her own self-image and self-worth. She let go of her fears of rejection and limitation and began seeing herself in ways that were fulfilling. She developed new skills, new attitudes, and became the friend that she wanted others to be to her.

What is your script telling you? Does your life reflect what you consistently say to yourself? Are you happy with the results? You can choose mediocrity or excellence. What are you bargaining for? It can all be yours if you take the action to make it happen.

There is a poem that I love by Jessie B. Rittenhouse, which I first saw in the book *Think and Grow Rich*, by Napoleon Hill. In the poem, she says, "I worked for a menial's hire, only to learn dismayed, that any wage I had asked of life, life would have paid." Think about that. You may still have to overcome some of your mind-sets and beliefs about the past, but stop working for a menial's hire. Life will give you anything that you desire and work to get.

Whenever my old scripts began to play in my mind, I had to start having a conversation with myself. I wrote out positive things for me to say. I would tell myself when thoughts of negativity hung around, "That is not my thought. My life matters. I am here for a purpose." Those thoughts do not reflect the real me. I was created to prosper; I was created to help others. I was created to succeed. I would then gather up a bunch of quotes from successful people and say them out loud. Find sources of inspiration for yourself. Have them in places where you can easily reach them. You never know when you may need one. They are rescue quotes when I need to remind myself that I am a champion. It's like refreshing your breath with a sweet mint.

Change what you are saying, seeing, and thinking about yourself. If you think and meditate about something long enough with energy and passion, you will eventually say it. If you continue to say it, you will have it. Start speaking powerful words to breathe life into your situation, your business, and over your family.

Write out your script. Writing it down will help you. Writing helps you clarify what it is you really want to do so that you can move forward. Read your script, your vision, and your goals for your life every day. Keep this in front of you. Reading your script daily will help to imprint this vision in your mind. It will create a burning desire that will help propel you to your next level.

You may think, "I have done all that stuff and it did not work." I would have to agree with you, but look at what your words just claimed for you—"not working." I want so much to inspire and motivate you to action. I have lived in those dead places where nothing good resulted from my efforts. I promise you that things will change for you. You will reach your next level. You have everything to gain.

State your vision out loud. Do something each day to move you forward. Find people who are doing what you want to do and contact them. You will be surprised at how many people will respond to you. Get up and get out. Life is in constant motion. Get into the motion.

Some people are collectors of information but never a doer of the information they collect. They read self-help books, attend seminars, and obtain certifications. Not taking action steps to implement what you have learned is utterly foolish and not serving you. I call that the Humpty Dumpty Syndrome. You are just sitting on a wall. Life is moving on, but, oh well, Humpty continues to sit. He sees what is going on in the world, but he still sits idly. He has a good view. He was content just sitting, and then his fall came. All the king's horses and all the king's men could not put Humpty Dumpty together again. Nelson Mandela said, "There is no passion to be found playing small—in settling for a life that is less than the one you are capable of living."

Many people are offended or turned off when someone quotes a scripture from the Bible. Yet these same people will quote Gandhi, Mother Teresa, Donald Trump, Confucius, Maya Angelou. A good quote is a good quote. If it helps you to get from point A to point B, use it. Don't allow yourself to get hung up on those things. The Bible says, "Out of the same mouth proceeds blessing and cursing" (James 3:10, KJV), so speak blessings to your life. Let this be your moment to live out the real script for your life. It will bless you and those around you.

CHAPTER 10

Forgiveness: The Key to Mastery

> Resentment is like drinking poison and then hoping it will kill your enemies.
>
> —*Nelson Mandela*

Forgiveness opens the door for true transformation and restoration in your life. It allows you to let go of your past (pain, failures, mistakes, wrongs) that was watered, fed, relived, edited, and nurtured by you. You have the right to let go, release, and be free from the past that did not serve you, that haunted you, that kept you in small places that did not restore and heal you.

Ask yourself, Is this thought serving me? Is it life restoring? Is thinking about this experience making my life better or worse? If it is making your life worse, release it. Take the high road.

* * *

In order to move forward, I had to learn to forgive. You know, I thought that all the people who hurt me in the past would have been punished, but guess what, they were not. I was sexually abused by someone who continued to live and prosper. But I was still living in the prison of hurt, shame, and wanting that person to take the blame. They had moved on; I did not.

You may recall that my mother and I did not see eye to eye. Perhaps I was a bit challenging for her as a single mom. She did not agree with the vision that I had for my life. During one argument, my mother said that she was doing the best she could. I replied, "Your best is not good enough." I wanted so desperately for us to have a better life. When my mother told me she hated that she had me, I internalized that and started to hate myself. But hate never wins; somebody always loses. Hating yourself sends out signals to people who could otherwise be instrumental in your growth and transformation in life and makes them turn away.

Over the years, I am glad to say that my relationship with my mother improved. Ultimately, she became my best friend and supported my choices in life. We were eventually able to celebrate each other's uniqueness. When my mother died, I was so thankful for the happy years we shared together while she was on this earth. I would still be living in regret if I had not made peace with her.

Not only did I forgive my mother and myself; I forgave all the people who out of their own ignorance had hurt me, and I am able to now embrace each new dawn with confidence and joy.

* * *

Forgiveness adds value to your life; you are no longer a victim.

If you stay in hate, you will lose. You may appear to have the upper hand, but really it is the hand that will keep you in a pit of despair. You do not want to hang out in that place. If you are reading this book, you are looking for more in your life. As you become better at loving yourself, forgiving others, and replacing your old beliefs and the programming that held you back, the more successful you will become.

In order to make changes that last, it takes courage and work to turn negating, self-defeating thoughts and pictures of yourself into positive, life-changing ones. You are worth all the effort and time that this takes. You will eventually feel better about yourself, and others will also see the positive changes in you. You will be blessed with good health, the right people in your life, good business success, freedom from depression and self-condemnation—a cornucopia of good things for you.

One of my favorite quotes on forgiveness comes from someone I admire greatly, Marianne Williamson. She says, "You can live the rest of your life reacting to and replaying what went before, but that won't serve you or deliver you. And everyone you meet will subconsciously know how you responded to your past. They will know whether you're stuck there or better for having been there."

If people do you wrong, forgive them. If your partner cheats on you, forgive your partner. Forgive the weakness in others. It can help them to heal as well.

> As I walked out the door toward the gate that would lead to my freedom, I knew if I didn't leave my bitterness and hatred behind, I'd still be in prison.
>
> —*Nelson Mandela*

CHAPTER 11

Complete Restoration Awaits You

> Greatness is not achieved by never falling but by rising each time we fall.
>
> —*Confucius*

There are two faces to failure: You missed the mark, stopped and gave up, and quit and lived quietly thereafter. Or, you missed the mark, reviewed your steps, decided to change your course, picked yourself up, reinvented yourself, and stepped into your true calling.

* * *

You may wonder how I arrived at a place of wholeness and fulfillment after coming from a place of self-hatred and wanting to harm myself.

No matter what obstacles I faced, even in my deepest despair, I was always seeking and searching for more. The old notions of not being good enough with no right to a fulfilling life ate away like hot acid inside of me.

So how did I go from A to Z? I found a teacher who was new to the Los Angeles area but not new to transforming her own life and helping others. That teacher was Louise Hay. I went to her home, I saw her and heard her story, and the teaching resonated within me. Everything that she imparted to me has remained with me. I love Louise and am so glad she came into my life. Louise and I shared many moments, and she taught me how to use affirmations. I was on the path, but the journey was not yet complete.

One day a friend invited me to her church for an event that she could not really describe. She said it was a program that had changed her life. I was not interested. But she continued to invite me, and eventually I broke down and went. The church was a small congregation, with approximately two hundred people. When I arrived, they were singing, and everyone appeared to be filled with joy. On the wall, I found their mission statement: "We are committed to leading the hurt and lost to complete restoration."

Huh? Complete restoration! I read it again. We are committed to leading the hurt and lost to complete restoration through the power of Jesus Christ. You will remember that my association with church and even at times God has been at odds. So how was this going to work? I was not sure, but I knew I had nothing to lose. By this time, I knew that recovery and reinvention of myself had to take place first in my life. I was tired of starting and stopping, gaining ground and losing ground. So I committed to enroll in the program and complete it. There is power in commitment!

I was able to allow God to heal the damage in my soul. I knew I could not do this, but God could. This was an enormous part of my process and journey. It was the place that anchored my soul and brought peace to my heart and mind. By allowing God to heal those wounds inside of me, it brought me to a place of overcoming—my opinion about God not loving me and my fear that God would block any attempts at lasting success and happiness because I had sinned.

With the help of an accountability coach, I was able to cancel the old beliefs, past abuse, addictions, bitterness, fear, self-harm, and betrayal. I had to forgive all the losses from my past and bitterness and release it to God. I had to let it go. I had to forgive the people and myself for not believing in me and not taking actions to change my life sooner. This was a necessary process to free myself to be open to the next phase of my life journey. It was not altogether easy, but it was totally freeing! I was free, free to be who God created me to be and to allow this process to restore me to completeness. I was free from the hurts, pain, and damage to my soul, free to make mistakes, to fail, and to know that *I* was not a mistake or a failure.

I was able to move from a place of brokenness to a place of peace and power. I was able to own my success and achievements and own the ability and talents that God created in me to help others move from a place of hopelessness or just mild mediocrity to a place of wholeness and success.

Where did all of this take me? It took me from a place of despair—the very pit of despair and darkness—to a place of overcoming and achievement where I could use the gifts that God gave me to better the world by helping others overcome their despair and hopelessness and to obtain peace, success, and confidence as well as financial gain in life.

* * *

Let me help you overcome your hopelessness. Here are some steps to successfully overcome your past and open the door to your future:

1. Recognize the damage, the lack (lack of happiness, success, health, peace, joy, fulfillment, recognition, acceptance, creativity, openness). Acknowledge it. See how the chain of past events has affected your life both positively and negatively.
2. Recognize that you and you alone are totally responsible for your life. There is no magic wand, and you cannot recreate yourself without help. For me, I had to recognize that I could not do this all by myself. Healing comes in relationships. For me, a new relationship with God was the beginning. Even though there is support in relationships, the buck stops here—it's all on me. Also, I had to recognize that just as God did not hold anything against me, I too, had to let go of all the *holds* I had on myself and others.

3. Release your past failures. Release the frustrations. Don't allow yourself to remain stuck. Embrace change. Use the pain in your life to transform your life. This will lead to a sense of fulfillment. The dots will all of a sudden connect. You'll wake up with joy in the morning. When a storm does come your way (something that you had not expected, a hiccup in your plans), that is OK. You'll move with passion and confidence, knowing that "this too shall pass."
4. Commit to your journey and your growth. Commit to moving forward. Commit to live life to the fullest. Commit to learning something new every day, every week, every month, and to learning how other people overcame their challenges. Be determined that nothing will deter you.
5. Take the time to invest wisely in yourself—financially, spiritually, emotionally, and intellectually. The person who succeeds is the person who never stops learning or growing. Age is not a factor in investing, learning, and growing.
6. Surround yourself with the right people—accountability partners, mastermind groups, support groups. They will help you on your road to reclaiming your life. If you're unhappy with where you are in your life, just take a look around. The people you've surrounded yourself with may be at the root of your problems. You will know when you are in the right place with the right people. Toxic people will choke the life out of you; toxic people create stress and strife that should be avoided at all costs. Healing comes through relationships with the right people who will help you reach your goals and celebrate you all along the way. One of the best quotes I have seen on mentoring is a quote by Lance Wallnau: "A mentor is someone who sees your potential when others do not. They speak to your future, and activate your launch on your journey of development. And it is your mentor who cares about both you and your high calling." This is how positive relationships with the right people will help you to heal, grow, and reach your potential.

7. As you grow in your new life, you will be able to help others along the way. Take the lessons that you've learned, and whenever you can, share them. You can now help others to feel the song inside of them. That is so powerful. You will be a positive force that has impact just by being.
8. Stop putting your life on hold. Begin today. Take some action now. Don't tell yourself, "When the children are grown, I'll take some time for myself." Or, "When I feel like I can make a difference, I will look for a new job or go back to school or attend a workshop." Or, "When I retire, then I will try to do something that I really love." Sometimes we wait our whole lives for a "when" that never comes. Your *when* must become your *now*. This will cause a shift in your thinking and actions. You will begin to value yourself more, and others will value you more as well.

As we let our own light shine, we unconsciously give other people permission to do the same.

—*Marianne Williamson*

A LETTER TO ME FROM LOUISE HAY

Nicole — Be "willing" to Forgive: the Universe will work out the "hows", & you will find peace of mind & True Freedom.

Happy Birthday
Laurie

CHAPTER 12

My Personal Creed

After all the changes and self-reflection, I've come up with a new creed for myself.

I believe with God's help, direction, and guidance, I can inspire, encourage, motivate, and help others who would otherwise give up on life—those who live defeated, die with their dream inside, or walk around in a place of deadness.

I have come from places of despair, pain, hopelessness, and deadness; I've made changes that have helped me escape a life of defeat and constantly wanting to die. Even though it has taken me a long time to be where I am, I have never put out the lamp on my dream.

I believe it is important to be surrounded by like-minded people and people who support and celebrate you. I have God, my coach, my family, and my friends. They believe in me and want the best for me. God wants me to prosper and fulfill his plan and purpose for me on this earth.

I believe that if others can do something, I can do it as well, and so can you. I know that if I can achieve something, whether or not I'm afraid, I'll stand as an example for someone who feels she or he cannot.

I believe that I am worthy of God's best in life. I believe that God holds nothing against me. God is not mad at me. God placed this passion in my heart to help others see and believe that their dreams are doable. Never give up.

* * *

I encourage you to write your own personal creed.

EPILOGUE

When I was first diagnosed with breast cancer, my relationship was ending. I was not the one calling it quits. My partner was. I went through cancer treatments all alone. To add to the pain, I was evicted from my apartment, my car was in need of serious repair, I did not have enough food to eat, emotionally I felt burned to the bones, and to top it off, my body had failed me and I was addicted to drugs.

I was seeking death because I was afraid of living. I did not really want to die, but I was living each day, each hour, minute, and second in pain. It really hurt just to be alive. If only I could lay my head down and fall into a deep sleep. If only I could close my eyes and wake up with a different set of circumstances—a new life, joy-filled days, and peaceful nights. I wanted a liberal dose of affection, caring friends who would not criticize my pain and my shame, and financial freedom. I wanted the unthinkable.

When one is in the throes of fighting for one's life, as I was when I attempted suicide, only that moment matters. If I pour boiling hot water on my foot, for the moment I do not have to worry about what someone else thinks about me. I have to attend to the emergency at hand.

When I look back over that period of my life, I can see the grace and favor of God. I can see his goodness and mercy. There was always a person around me, someone to help slow me down or turn me around, but when I think about it, all the people in my life contributed something.

You may feel you do not deserve more, but you do. You will have to initiate the help, and it may be trial and error at first, but you will find the right support.

If you are hurting right now, if you are thinking about hurting yourself, call out for help. Find a place, club, group, church, mastermind group, or form your own. Fight for your life! You are worth it!

APPENDIX A

Inspiration

When nothing else works, try this:

> "The greatest failure in life is to stop trying."
> —*Napoleon Hill*

> "There is always a way for you to change; never stop trying."
> —*Neecol Resnin*

I had to start having a conversation with myself. When thoughts of negativity hung around, I would tell myself, "That is not my thought." I would gather up a bunch of quotes from successful people and say them out loud. Find sources of inspiration for yourself. Have them in places where you can easily reach them. You never know when you may need one. They are rescue quotes to remind you that you are a champion. Here are some to get you started.

One Hundred Quotes to Inspire You

1. "If you want to achieve greatness stop asking for permission."
   —*Anonymous*
2. "Things work out best for those who make the best of how things work out."
   —*John Wooden*

3. "To live a creative life, we must lose our fear of being wrong."
   —*Anonymous*
4. "If you are not willing to risk the usual, you will have to settle for the ordinary."
   —*Jim Rohn*
5. "Trust because you are willing to accept the risk, not because it's safe or certain."
   —*Anonymous*
6. "Take up one idea. Make that one idea your life—think of it, dream of it, live on that idea. Let the brain, muscles, nerves, every part of your body, be full of that idea, and just leave every other idea alone. This is the way to *success*."
   —*Swami Vivekananda*
7. "All our dreams can come true if we have the courage to pursue them."
   —*Walt Disney*
8. "Good things come to people who wait, but better things come to those who go out and get them."
   —*Anonymous*
9. "If you do what you always did, you will get what you always got."
   —*Anonymous*
10. "Success is walking from failure to failure with no loss of enthusiasm."
    —*Winston Churchill*
11. "Just when the caterpillar thought the world was ending, he turned into a butterfly."
    —*Proverb*
12. "Successful *entrepreneurs* are givers and not takers of positive energy."
    —*Anonymous*
13. "Whenever you see a *successful person* you only see the public glories, never the private sacrifices to reach them."
    —*Vaibhav Shah*
14. "Opportunities don't happen, you create them."
    —*Chris Grosser*

15. "Try not to become a *person of success*, but rather try to become a person of value."
   —Albert Einstein
16. "Great minds discuss ideas; average minds discuss events; small minds discuss people."
   —Eleanor Roosevelt
17. "I have not failed. I've just found 10,000 ways that won't work."
   —Thomas A. Edison
18. "If you don't value your time, neither will others. Stop giving away your time and talents—start charging for it."
   —Kim Garst
19. "A successful man is one who can lay a firm foundation with the bricks others have thrown at him."
   —David Brinkley
20. "No one can make you feel inferior without your consent."
   —Eleanor Roosevelt
21. "The whole secret of a successful life is to find out what is one's destiny to do, and then do it."
   —Henry Ford
22. "If you're going through hell, keep going."
   —Winston Churchill
23. "The ones who are crazy enough to think they can change the world are the ones who do."
   —Anonymous
24. "Don't raise your voice, improve your argument."
   —Anonymous
25. "What seems to us as bitter trials are often blessings in disguise."
   —Oscar Wilde
26. "The meaning of life is to find your gift. The purpose of life is to give it away."
   —Anonymous
27. "The distance between insanity and genius is measured only by success."
   —Bruce Feirstein

28. "When you stop chasing the wrong things, you give the right things a chance to catch you."
   —*Lolly Daskal*
29. "Don't be afraid to give up the good to go for the great."
   —*John D. Rockefeller*
30. "No masterpiece was ever created by a lazy artist."
   —*Anonymous*
31. "Happiness is a butterfly, which when pursued, is always beyond your grasp, but which, if you will sit down quietly, may alight upon you."
   —*Nathaniel Hawthorne*
32. "If you can't explain it simply, you don't understand it well enough."
   —*Albert Einstein*
33. "Blessed are those who can give without remembering and take without forgetting."
   —*Anonymous*
35. "What's the point of being alive if you don't at least try to do something remarkable."
   —*Anonymous*
36. "Life is not about finding yourself. Life is about creating yourself."
   —*Lolly Daskal*
37. "Nothing in the world is more common than unsuccessful people with talent."
   —*Anonymous*
38. "Knowledge is being aware of what you can do. Wisdom is knowing when not to do it."
   —*Anonymous*
39. "Your problem isn't the problem. Your reaction is the problem."
   —*Anonymous*
40. "You can do anything, but not everything."
   —*Anonymous*
41. "Innovation distinguishes between a leader and a follower."
   —*Steve Jobs*

42. "There are two types of people who will tell you that you cannot make a difference in this world: those who are afraid to try and those who are afraid you will succeed."
—*Ray Goforth*
43. "Thinking should become your capital asset, no matter whatever ups and downs you come across in your life."
—*A. P. J. Abdul Kalam*
44. "I find that the harder I work, the more luck I seem to have."
—*Thomas Jefferson*
45. "The starting point of all achievement is desire."
—*Napoleon Hill*
46. "Success is the sum of small efforts, repeated day-in and day-out."
—*Robert Collier*
47. "If you want to achieve excellence, you can get there today. As of this second, quit doing less-than-excellent work."
—*Thomas J. Watson*
48. "All progress takes place outside the comfort zone."
—*Michael John Bobak*
49. "You may only succeed if you desire *succeeding*; you may only fail if you do not mind failing."
—*Philippos*
50. "Courage is resistance to fear, mastery of fear—not absence of fear."
—*Mark Twain*
51. "Only put off until tomorrow what you are willing to die having left undone."
—*Pablo Picasso*
52. "People often say that motivation doesn't last. Well, neither does bathing—that's why we recommend it daily."
—*Zig Ziglar*
53. "We become what we think about most of the time, and that's the strangest secret."
—*Earl Nightingale*
54. "The only place where success comes before work is in the dictionary."
—*Vidal Sassoon*

55. "The best reason to start an organization is to make meaning; to create a product or service to make the world a better place."
—Guy Kawasaki
56. "I find that when you have a real interest in life and a curious life, sleep is not the most important thing."
—Martha Stewart
57. "It's not what you look at that matters; it's what you see."
—Anonymous
58. "The road to success and the road to failure are almost exactly the same."
—Colin R. Davis
59. "The function of leadership is to produce more leaders, not more followers."
—Ralph Nader
60. "Success is liking yourself, liking what you do, and liking how you do it."
—Maya Angelou
61. "As we look ahead into the next century, leaders will be those who empower others."
—Bill Gates
62. "A real entrepreneur is somebody who has no safety net underneath them."
—Henry Kravis
63. "The first step toward success is taken when you refuse to be a captive of the environment in which you first find yourself."
—Mark Caine
64. "People who succeed have momentum. The more they succeed, the more they want to succeed, and the more they find a way to succeed. Similarly, when someone is failing, the tendency is to get on a downward spiral that can even become a self-fulfilling prophecy."
—Tony Robbins
65. "When I dare to be powerful, to use my strength in the service of my vision, then it becomes less and less important whether I am afraid."
—Audre Lorde

66. "Whenever you find yourself on the side of the majority, it is time to pause and reflect."
—*Mark Twain*
67. "The successful warrior is the average man with laser-like focus."
—*Bruce Lee*
68. "Courage is resistance to fear, mastery of fear—not absence of fear."
—*Mark Twain*
69. "Develop success from failures. Discouragement and failure are two of the surest stepping stones to success."
—*Dale Carnegie*
70. "If you don't design your own life plan, chances are you'll fall into someone else's plan. And guess what they have planned for you? Not much."
—*Jim Rohn*
71. "If you genuinely want something, don't wait for it—teach yourself to be impatient."
—*Gurbaksh Chahal*
72. "Don't let the fear of losing be greater than the excitement of winning."
—*Robert Kiyosaki*
73. "If you want to make a permanent change, stop focusing on the size of your problems and start focusing on the size of you!"
—*T. Harv Eker*
74. "You can't connect the dots looking forward; you can only connect them looking backwards. So you have to trust that the dots will somehow connect in your future. You have to trust in something—your gut, destiny, life, karma, whatever. This approach has never let me down, and it has made all the difference in my life."
—*Steve Jobs*
75. "Successful people do what unsuccessful people are not willing to do. Don't wish it were easier, wish you were better."
—*Jim Rohn*

76. "The number one reason people fail in life is because they listen to their friends, family, and neighbors."
   —*Napoleon Hill*
77. "The reason most people never reach their goals is that they don't define them, or ever seriously consider them as believable or achievable. Winners can tell you where they are going, what they plan to do along the way, and who will be sharing the adventure with them."
   —*Denis Waitley*
78. "In my experience, there is only one motivation, and that is desire. No reasons or principle contain it or stand against it."
   —*Jane Smiley*
79. "Success does not consist in never making mistakes but in never making the same one a second time."
   —*George Bernard Shaw*
80. "I don't want to get to the end of my life and find that I lived just the length of it. I want to have lived the width of it as well."
   —*Diane Ackerman*
81. "You must expect great things of yourself before you can do them."
   —*Michael Jordan*
82. "Motivation is what gets you started. Habit is what keeps you going."
   —*Jim Ryun*
83. "People rarely succeed unless they have fun in what they are doing."
   —*Dale Carnegie*
84. "There is no chance, no destiny, no fate, that can hinder or control the firm resolve of a determined soul."
   —*Ella Wheeler Wilcox*
85. "Our greatest fear should not be of failure but of succeeding at things in life that don't really matter."
   —*Francis Chan*
86. "You've got to get up every morning with determination if you're going to go to bed with satisfaction."
   —*George Lorimer*

87. "To be successful you must accept all challenges that come your way. You can't just accept the ones you like."
—*Mike Gafka*
88. "Success is . . . knowing your purpose in life, growing to reach your maximum potential, and sowing seeds that benefit others."
—*John C. Maxwell*
89. "Be miserable. Or motivate yourself. Whatever has to be done, it's always your choice."
—*Wayne Dyer*
90. "To accomplish great things, we must not only act, but also dream, not only plan, but also believe."
—*Anatole France*
91. "Most of the important things in the world have been accomplished by people who have kept on trying when there seemed to be no help at all."
—*Dale Carnegie*
92. "You measure the size of the accomplishment by the obstacles you had to overcome to reach your goals."
—*Booker T. Washington*
93. "Real difficulties can be overcome; it is only the imaginary ones that are unconquerable."
—*Theodore N. Vail*
94. "It is better to fail in originality than to succeed in imitation."
—*Herman Melville*
95. "Fortune sides with him who dares."
—*Virgil*
96. "Little minds are tamed and subdued by misfortune; but great minds rise above it."
—*Washington Irving*
97. "Failure is the condiment that gives success its flavor."
—*Truman Capote*
98. "Don't let what you cannot do interfere with what you can do."
—*John R. Wooden*
99. "You may have to fight a battle more than once to win it."
—*Margaret Thatcher*

100. "A man can be as great as he wants to be. If you believe in yourself and have the courage, the determination, the dedication, the competitive drive and if you are willing to sacrifice the little things in life and pay the price for the things that are worthwhile, it can be done."
—*Vince Lombardi*

Quotes for Entrepreneurs

1. "I intend to be the richest man in the world."
—*Howard Hughes*
2. "To be successful, you must act big, think big, and talk big."
—*Aristotle Onassis*
3. "It is my utmost desire to become a billionaire in my lifetime and also give away billions of dollars. I don't think any paid employment on earth can help me achieve that dream. If I become a billionaire in my lifetime, I will just be another self-made entrepreneur on the list. But if I don't, I will die knowing I gave that dream my best shot."
—*Ajaero Tony Martins*
4. "Like success, failure is many things to many people. With positive mental attitude, failure is a learning experience, a rung on the ladder, and a plateau at which to get your thoughts in order to prepare to try again."
—*W. Clement Stone*
5. "Out of the abundance of the heart, the mouth speaks."
—*Matthew 12:34, NKJV*
6. "Be careful of your thoughts, for they may break into words."
—*Anonymous*
7. "I like thinking big. If you're going to be thinking anything, you might as well think big."
—*Donald Trump*
8. "We are self-made or never made."
—*Dr. Sidney Newton*

9. "I am looking for a lot of men who have the infinite capacity to not know what can't be done."
   —Henry Ford
10. "I'm not afraid of turning eighty and I have lots of things to do. I don't have time for dying."
    —Ingvar Kamprad
11. "What's the worst that could happen? Everyone turned me down; big deal."
    —J. K. Rowling
12. "Don't limit yourself. Many people limit themselves to what they think they can do. You can go as far as your mind lets you. What you believe, remember you can achieve."
    —Mary Kay Ash
13. "I always knew I was destined for greatness."
    —Oprah Winfrey
14. "Every tomorrow has two handles. You can take hold of the handle of anxiety or the handle of enthusiasm. Upon your choice, so will be the day."
    —Brian Tracy
15. "There are no mistakes in life, just learning opportunities."
    —Robert Kiyosaki
16. "As [a man] thinketh in his heart, so is he."
    —Proverbs 23:7, KJV
17. "I have never run into a guy who could win at the top level in anything today and didn't have the right attitude; didn't give it everything he had, at least while he was doing it; wasn't prepared; and didn't have the whole program worked out."
    —Ted Turner
18. "I always knew I was going to be rich. I don't think I ever doubted it for a minute."
    —Warren Buffett
19. "Be courageous. I have seen many depressions in business. Always, America has emerged from these stronger and more prosperous. Be brave as your fathers before you. Have faith! Go forward."
    —Thomas Edison

20. "Getting rich begins with the right mind-set, the right words, and the right plan."
—*Robert Kiyosaki*
21. "I am black; I don't feel burdened by it and I don't think it's a huge responsibility. It's part of who I am. It does not define me."
—*Oprah Winfrey*
22. "We have a problem. 'Congratulations.' But it's a tough problem. 'Then double congratulations.'"
—*W. Clement Stone*
23. "Life and death are in the power of the tongue."
—*Proverbs 18:21, KJV*
25. "The greatest discovery of all time is that a person can change by merely changing his attitude."
—*Oprah Winfrey*
26. "Self-suggestion makes you master of yourself."
—*W. Clement Stone*
27. "Do you know that within your power lies every step you ever dreamed of stepping and within your power lies every joy you ever dreamed of seeing? Within yourself lies everything you ever dreamed of being. Become everything that God wants you to be. It is within your reach. Dare to grow into your dreams and claim this as your motto: Let it be me."
—*Mary Kay Ash*
28. "I don't think of myself as a poor, deprived ghetto girl who made good. I think of myself as somebody who from an early age knew I was responsible for myself, and I had to make good."
—*Oprah Winfrey*
29. "A man is what he thinks all day long."
—*Ralph Waldo Emerson*
30. "Nothing can stop a man with the right mental attitude from achieving his goals, and nothing on earth can help a man with the wrong mental attitude."
—*Thomas Jefferson*

Use these to help inspire and motivate you. It works if you work it.

APPENDIX B

Resources for Recovering from Addiction

The following list is to help get you started and is taken from the Addiction Recovery Guide website (www.addictionrecoveryguide.org).

Alcoholics Anonymous (AA)

www.aa.org
This is a twelve-step program for people in recovery from alcohol abuse. The site provides an online list of central offices and groups in the United States and Canada, meeting contact information, a description of the twelve steps and traditions, a listing of AA literature, and a bulletin board.

All Addictions Anonymous

www.alladdictionsanonymous.com
All Addictions Anonymous focuses solely on the twelve-step program and how to work the steps. They allow only brief personal sharing about "war stories" in order to illustrate patterns of addiction and do not explore psychological issues. The program connects suffering addicts to recovered addicts who guide newcomers through a personalized one-on-one study of the original twelve-step program described in the Big Book of Alcoholics Anonymous. The program is open to people with any addiction.

Go to the Contact Us section and leave a confidential message on their 24-hour pager: 416-468-8603 or send an e-mail. You will be contacted and connected with someone in your area, or arrangements will be made to get you help by phone.

Big Book Sponsorship

www.bigbooksponsorship.org
The purpose of this site is to show people recovering from all addictions precisely how to recover using the Big Book of AA. It provides information about the original AA program that produced recovery rates that were 50–75 percent successful and information resources on who, where, why, what, and how to use the Big Book and its methodology for facilitating spiritual experiences that enable the addict to recover. The site helps connect people with Big Book sponsors who practice the original program format.

Cocaine Anonymous (CA)

www.ca.org
This twelve-step program is for people in recovery from cocaine and other drugs. The site describes the twelve steps and traditions and provides a self-test, a meeting starter kit, and CA literature. Under "Local Phones and Links," referral phone numbers are listed by location in the United States, with contact numbers provided for Canada, the United Kingdom, and the Netherlands as well. To participate in online meetings, click on "Online, All Locations" at the end of the referral list.

Crystal Meth Anonymous (CMA)

www.crystalmeth.org
This twelve-step program is for people in recovery from crystal meth amphetamine and other related drugs. Based on the twelve-step model, the website includes basic information on the CMA

fellowship, the twelve traditions, CMA meeting schedules, and information on how to start a meeting.

Marijuana Anonymous World Services

www.marijuana-anonymous.org
Marijuana Anonymous uses the basic twelve-step recovery program founded by Alcoholics Anonymous. Their website covers the twelve steps and the twelve traditions, online pamphlets on various aspects of marijuana addiction, a meeting directory by geographic area, and a list of online meetings.

Methadone Anonymous Support

www.methadonesupport.org
This is a twelve-step program for people using methadone in recovery from opiate addiction. The site provides an online meeting locator by state, methadone discussion lists, online meetings, a news section, a description of the twelve steps and traditions, and information on HIV, Hepatitis C, and buprenorphine.

Narcotics Anonymous World Services (NA)

www.na.org
This twelve-step recovery program from addiction to drugs is based on the Alcoholics Anonymous model. The site provides basic information on the program and NA literature.

Nicotine Anonymous

www.nicotine-anonymous.org
Nicotine Anonymous is a twelve-step fellowship program based on the recovery program of Alcoholics Anonymous. Their website has a meeting locator by state or country and online information in English and five other languages.

Pills Anonymous

www.pillsanonymous.com
This website is geared to the needs of those recovering from prescription drug addiction. It discusses the twelve-step traditions and includes sample stories and a meeting locator.

Recoveries Anonymous

www.r-a.org
Recoveries Anonymous (RA) is a recovery fellowship that uses the twelve steps for a "solution-focused program of recovery." It welcomes anyone with any kind of problem or self-destructive behavior, including family and friends and those who are looking for spiritual growth. The goal of RA is to "restore one's sanity," not simply to maintain abstinence. Their website provides background information on their approach as well as a meeting locator and information on how to start a group. Free online recovery guides are available, along with downloadable PDF versions of RA's solution-focused books (with a small contribution requested).

APPENDIX C

My Tips for Coping with Breast Cancer

Breast cancer is the most common cancer among women worldwide and the second-most common cancer overall. In 2015, an estimated 231,840 cases of invasive breast cancer will be diagnosed in the United States alone. So no matter who you are or where you live, understanding breast cancer is important. There are many great sites that will give you tons of information.

A word of caution for anyone who has been newly diagnosed with breast cancer. Searching the Internet for breast cancer will bring up volumes of information. Some of the information may seem somewhat contradictory, and some of the information is just overwhelming. Get a second opinion from a different doctor if you are unsure. Getting a second and third opinion never hurts.

These tips will help you cope:

- Once you have decided which doctor you will go to for your treatments, quiz them. Take a list of questions to your visit. You need to feel confident about the doctor you select. There are no dumb questions.
- Call family and friends early in the process so that you can have support.
- Let your employer know what is going on and how much time you will need off work. I have a friend who just took some vacation time when she had her surgery but worked while she was receiving treatment. I did

take some time off work when I had cancer in 1989, which included radiation and chemotherapy. However, I worked every day when I received radiation treatment for my second bout with cancer.
- You may lose your hair to chemotherapy; be sure you shop around early for wigs and hair wraps. Many women do not use wigs or hair wraps or caps; they feel comfortable to have a bald head. Do whatever makes you most comfortable.
- Never feel shy about asking for help. People are there for you, and survivors are really glad to be supportive.
- Pay attention to nutrition—it's really important and can be a life changer. Exercise when you are able to; rest when you need to. It will make you feel better.
- Many hospitals and oncologists have a list of resources. When you begin your treatment, you will meet other people who will also have resources.

Resources

American Cancer Society: www.cancer.org
National Breast Cancer Foundation:
    www.nationalbreastcancer.org
National Cancer Institute: www.cancer.gov

www.ingramcontent.com/pod-product-compliance
Lightning Source LLC
Chambersburg PA
CBHW071724020426
42333CB00017B/2379